THE ART OF EMBRACING

NOTHINGNESS

By
Robert J Glen

DEDICATION

This book is dedicated to those who seek solace in stillness and find strength in the quiet spaces of life, to those who embrace the art of letting go and discover freedom in release, and to all who dare to explore the fertile ground of nothingness, finding creativity and growth in the void.

May you find peace, inspiration, and profound fulfillment in the spaces between.

TABLE OF CONTENTS

INTRODUCTION

In a world constantly in motion, filled with endless noise and relentless demands, the concepts of silence, nothingness, and letting go often seem counterintuitive. Yet, within these seemingly empty or absent spaces lie profound opportunities for growth, creativity, and fulfillment. This book delves into these transformative concepts, exploring how embracing moments of stillness and emptiness can lead to a richer, more meaningful life. Together, these themes form a compelling narrative about the value of stillness, the power of letting go, and the creative potential inherent in nothingness. By exploring these concepts, this book invites you to embrace the spaces in between, allowing them to enrich your life in unexpected and profound ways.

CHAPTER 1
The Art of Emracing Nothingness

Exploring the concept of nothingness reveals a fascinating and often misunderstood aspect of our existence. Far from being a mere void or absence, nothingness can be perceived as a fertile ground for endless possibilities. When we shift our perspective to see empty spaces not as lacking but as opportunities brimming with potential, our understanding of nothingness transforms. This first chapter encourages us to reframe our perception of emptiness, viewing it as a blank canvas that invites creativity and innovation. By appreciating the beauty within nothingness, we can uncover its hidden strengths and tap into resources we might otherwise overlook.

Throughout this chapter, we will delve into various dimensions of nothingness and how they contribute to personal growth and development. We will examine how embracing nothingness can create an environment conducive to brainstorming and self-reflection, allowing us to reconnect with our inner thoughts and self-determined calmness. The chapter will highlight existing practices such as minimalism and meditation that help clear away distractions and make room for new ideas. Additionally, we will briefly explore philosophical perspectives that shed light on the interconnectedness and transformative power of nothingness. By the end of this chapter, readers will gain a deeper appreciation for the multifaceted nature of nothingness and its potential as a catalyst for creativity and advanced personal advancement.

Reframing Nothingness

Nothingness, often misconstrued as a mere void or absence, can be reimagined as a pristine or blank canvas ready for new possibilities. This perspective transformation is foundational in appreciating how nothingness acts as an incubator for potential. When we perceive an empty space, we should not see it as lacking, but rather as brimming with opportunities waiting to be realized. Imagine walking into an empty room; instead of focusing on the absence of furniture or decorations, envision the endless ways it could be transformed to reflect your creativity and innovation.

Taking a step further, we observe that this blank slate invites us to project our own ideas and dreams onto it. Whether it's an artist staring at an empty canvas or a writer facing a blank page, the initial state of nothingness offers a non-threatening environment to experiment, make mistakes, and ultimately grow. It's in these untouched spaces where imagination runs wild and previously unconsidered possibilities come to light.

The freedom from pre-existing patterns or distractions allows for a raw and unfiltered exploration of one's creativity.

Guidelines for harnessing this potential in everyday life include intentionally setting aside spaces and moments that are free from clutter and distraction. By doing so, we create environments conducive to brainstorming and personal reflection. This practice helps individuals to reconnect with their inner thoughts and develop fresh perspectives. It may be as simple as taking a walk in a quiet park or spending a few minutes in silent meditation each day.

Moreover, recognizing the potential for creativity and imagination within nothingness enriches our understanding of its value. In moments of stillness and quietude, our minds have the chance to wander and explore uncharted territories. This is not about passive idleness but rather about active engagement with the subconscious mind, which can lead to breakthroughs and innovations. Many great thinkers and inventors have attributed their moments of clarity and inspiration to periods of solitude and silence.

For instance, renowned physicist Albert Einstein often spoke about the importance of imagination over knowledge. His revolutionary ideas about the nature of the universe came during times of introspection and contemplation. Similarly, numerous artists find their muse when they allow themselves the luxury of undistracted thought. These examples underscore the hidden potential within what might initially appear as nothingness.

A practical approach to nurture this creativity is to regularly schedule time away from the noise and busyness of daily life. Set aside intervals in your routine dedicated to quiet reflection, and carry a notebook to jot down any spontaneous ideas or insights that arise. Over time, this habit can help you tap into deeper layers of creativity and foster a more innovative mindset.

Viewing nothingness as a pathway to personal growth and mastery further exemplifies its positive force. The journey towards self-improvement often begins with a phase of clearing out the old to make way for the new. This concept parallels the idea of nothingness serving as a preparatory stage for personal development. When we strip away external distractions and excess, we create room to focus on what truly matters, be it our skills, relationships, or well-being.

Consider the practice of minimalism, which emphasizes simplifying one's surroundings to amplify personal fulfillment. By removing unnecessary possessions and commitments, individuals can concentrate their energy on pursuits that genuinely resonate with their values and aspirations. This intentional embrace of nothingness paves the way for achieving greater clarity, purpose, and mastery in various aspects of life.

Embracing this approach involves periodic evaluations of one's activities and possessions, ensuring they contribute meaningfully to personal growth. Decluttering both physical and mental spaces can be liberating, fostering a sense of calm and heightened focus. This ongoing process of shedding the superfluous allows for continuous self-discovery and progression towards one's goals.

Challenging the traditional perception of nothingness as merely a void or absence is crucial in reshaping our attitudes toward it. Historically, nothingness has been viewed through a lens of negativity, associated with lack, emptiness, and despair. However, by redefining nothingness as a fertile ground for new possibilities, we can shift this narrative towards a more empowering outlook.

This reevaluation calls for a change in mindset. Instead of equating nothingness with disadvantage or deficiency, recognize its inherent potential and beauty. Just as a sculptor sees a block of marble not as a mere stone but as a raw form teeming with artistic potential, we too can view empty spaces and quiet moments as opportunities for creation and growth.

Contemporary society often bombards us with stimuli and information, leaving little room for introspection and serenity. By consciously embracing and celebrating moments of nothingness, we reclaim a sense of balance and peace. This shift not only enhances our individual well-being but also contributes to a broader cultural appreciation of simplicity and tranquility.

Philosophical Perspectives on Nothingness

Eastern philosophies have long grappled with the concept of nothingness, emphasizing interconnectedness and the liberation from attachments. In Buddhism, for example, the idea of Śūnyatā or "emptiness" is a central tenet. This philosophy posits that all phenomena are void of intrinsic existence and emphasizes the importance of understanding this emptiness to attain enlightenment. By recognizing that everything is interconnected and impermanent, practitioners can liberate themselves from the cycle of suffering caused by attachment and aversion.

Taoism offers another perspective on nothingness, often symbolized through the concept of the Tao, which can be seen as the underlying order of the universe that is both beyond and within all things. The Tao Te Ching, attributed to Laozi, describes how embracing nothingness can lead to a harmonious life.

By letting go of rigid structures and beliefs, one can flow more naturally with the rhythms of life, leading to a state of peace and balance. This acceptance of nothingness doesn't signify a void but rather an open potential for growth and transformation.

In Zen Buddhism, practices like Zazen meditation focus on experiencing the present moment devoid of preconceived notions and attachments. Through mindfulness and meditation, individuals can experience a profound sense of emptiness, not as a lack but as a space of potential and awareness. This meditative practice encourages practitioners to witness their thoughts and feelings without clinging to them, thereby realizing the freedom that comes from embracing nothingness.

Existentialist viewpoints offer a starkly different yet equally profound interpretation of nothingness. This philosophical approach centers on individual responsibility and the creation of meaning in life, particularly in the perceived absence of inherent meaning. Jean-Paul Sartre famously asserted that "existence precedes essence," meaning that humans first exist and then define themselves through actions and choices. In this light, nothingness becomes the canvas upon which individuals must paint their own significance.

Sartre's concept of "the void" represents the emptiness within each person that fuels a perpetual search for meaning. This existential vacuum can prompt anxiety, known as "existential angst," due to the burden of freedom and choice. However, facing this nothingness also provides the opportunity for authentic living. By acknowledging the absence of predetermined purpose, individuals can take full ownership of their lives and create personal meaning, thus transforming the void into a source of empowerment.

Another key figure in existentialism, Albert Camus, explored the absurdity of life and the human struggle to find inherent value in a seemingly indifferent universe. In works like "The Myth of Sisyphus," Camus argued that one must imagine Sisyphus happy even as he endures endless, futile labor. Here, nothingness is not a barrier but a challenge to affirm life through conscious rebellion and the continuous quest for personal meaning amidst the absurd.

Ancient schools of thought provide further nuanced interpretations of existence, reality, and consciousness that enrich our understanding of nothingness. For instance, in Ancient Greek philosophy, the pre-Socratic thinker Parmenides argued that nothingness cannot exist because it is by definition the absence of existence. This paradoxical stance compelled later philosophers to delve into the nature of being and non-being, ultimately influencing many ontological studies.

Plato also touched upon nothingness but framed it within the context of forms and ideals. According to Plato, the material world is only a shadow of the true reality, which exists in the realm of forms. While this might imply a certain negation of physical existence, it also elevates the importance of intellectual and spiritual pursuits. Nothingness, in this regard, can be seen as the transient nature of the physical world contrasted against the enduring truth of the ideal forms.

Further eastward, Indian philosophy, particularly in the Advaita Vedanta tradition, discusses the concept of

"Maya" or illusion, which obscures the true nature of the self and reality. In this framework, nothingness is tied to the dissolution of illusions that bind the individual soul to the cycle of birth and rebirth. By transcending Maya, one can realize "Brahman," the ultimate reality that underlies all existence. Here, the acknowledgment of nothingness leads to a profound spiritual awakening and the unity of the self with the cosmos.

Investigating diverse insights into the human experience through the lens of emptiness and impermanence reveals common threads and distinct variations. In Buddhist teachings, the impermanence of life is a fundamental concept. Recognizing the transient nature of all things fosters a deeper appreciation for the present moment and encourages detachment from worldly desires. This view suggests that embracing impermanence can lead to a more meaningful and liberated existence.

Japanese aesthetics, particularly the concept of "wabi-sabi," embraces the beauty of imperfection and transience. Wabi-sabi finds elegance in the ephemeral and the incomplete, celebrating the natural cycles of growth and decay. This cultural appreciation for emptiness and impermanence teaches us to find beauty in the fleeting and to embrace the simplicity of existence. It is an invitation to live mindfully and cherish the small, often overlooked moments of life.

Cultural Descriptions of Nothingness

Different domains describe nothingness in unique and fascinating ways. In philosophy, nothingness is often explored through existentialism. Existentialists like Jean-Paul Sartre considered nothingness as a central element of human existence, emphasizing the void that can fill our lives when we recognize the absence of inherent meaning. This encounter with nothingness can be daunting, but it also presents an opportunity for individuals to create their own essence and purpose. Thus, from a philosophical standpoint, nothingness serves as a blank slate on which personal significance is inscribed.

In poetry, nothingness frequently manifests as an artistic device to explore deeper emotions and thoughts. Poets use silence and emptiness not merely as backdrops but as active components of their work. For instance, the pauses between lines or stanzas can evoke a sense of longing or contemplation, encouraging readers to ponder what lies in those gaps. Nothingness becomes a space for reflection, offering a stark contrast to the flood of words and emotions typically present in poetic expression. The use of nothingness in poetry exemplifies its ability to invoke profound introspection and emotional resonance.

Art, too, captures the essence of nothingness through minimalist approaches. Artists like Kazimir Malevich and his Black Square painting present the idea of nothingness visually. Such works strip away the excess, focusing on simplicity to convey complex ideas about existence and the void. In abstract art, the empty spaces are just as significant as the filled areas, challenging viewers to engage with the unseen and unspoken aspects of the artwork. Here, nothingness transforms into an integral part of the visual narrative, urging observers to find meaning within the absence.

Short stories often depict profound silence and letting go as key themes associated with nothingness. These narratives delve into characters' experiences of emptiness, whether it's the silence following a significant life event or the act of releasing past burdens. For example, in Ernest Hemingway's "A Clean, Well-Lighted Place," the quiet conversations and the tranquil setting emphasize the characters' inner turmoil and search for meaning amidst nothingness. This portrayal highlights how silence can be both a source of comfort and a reminder of existential isolation.

The theme of letting go is also prevalent in short stories, shedding light on the transformative power of embracing nothingness. Characters who relinquish attachments or confront deep-seated fears often undergo significant personal growth. Through such narratives, readers gain insight into the liberating aspect of letting go, understanding that nothingness isn't solely about absence but also about potential. This exploration encourages a shift in perspective, viewing emptiness as an opportunity rather than a deficit.

Mindfulness, meditation, and introspection provide practical ways to engage with nothingness. Mindfulness practices emphasize being present in the moment, allowing individuals to experience the full depth of their current state without attachment or judgment. This approach fosters a sense of peace and acceptance, acknowledging the voids within our minds and hearts as natural parts of the human experience. By focusing on the present, mindfulness helps individuals embrace nothingness and find tranquility in its simplicity.

Meditation offers another pathway to connect with nothingness. Through meditative practices, individuals learn to quiet their minds, gradually stripping away the incessant chatter and distractions of daily life. This process leads to an encounter with the vast, silent expanse of the mind, where nothingness resides. Meditation teaches us to sit with this emptiness, recognizing it as a space for renewal and clarity. By cultivating this practice, individuals can tap into the restorative power of nothingness, finding balance and insight in the process.

Introspection further deepens our engagement with nothingness. Reflecting on our thoughts, feelings, and experiences allows us to peel back layers and confront the empty spaces within ourselves. This self-examination often reveals underlying truths, fostering a more profound understanding of our innermost selves. By embracing introspection, we can navigate the contours of nothingness, transforming it into a realm of self-discovery and growth.

To truly navigate and embrace the concept of nothingness, foundational tools can be invaluable. One such tool is the practice of conscious breathing. Focusing on the breath anchors individuals in the present moment, providing a tangible connection to the here and now. This simple yet powerful technique helps calm the mind and opens the door to experiencing nothingness without fear or resistance.

Conscious breathing serves as a bridge, guiding us gently into the stillness and quietude of nothingness.

Another foundational tool is journaling, which enables individuals to document their thoughts and feelings about nothingness. Writing down these reflections helps clarify one's understanding and relationship with emptiness. It provides a safe space to explore and articulate the nuances of nothingness, turning abstract concepts into concrete insights. Journaling can become a cherished practice, offering continuous support on the journey toward embracing nothingness.

Visualization exercises also play a crucial role in this exploration. Imagining oneself in a place of serene emptiness—such as a vast, open plain or a tranquil sea—can help internalize the concept of nothingness. These mental images foster a sense of peace and acceptance, allowing individuals to visualize and emotionally connect with the idea of nothingness. Over time, these exercises cultivate familiarity and comfort with emptiness, transforming it from an unknown territory into a wellspring of potential and serenity.

The Allure of Unoccupied Spaces

Empty spaces hold a unique magnetism, drawing us towards them with an almost mystical allure. From the vastness of the cosmos to the desolate beauty of empty terrains, there is an undeniable charm in these unoccupied expanses. When we gaze into the night sky, dotted with countless stars against the backdrop of infinite darkness, we are reminded of our small place in the grand scheme of the universe. This humbling experience can evoke a sense of wonder and curiosity about what lies beyond, offering an opportunity to connect with something larger than ourselves.

Similarly, desolate landscapes like deserts and wide open plains can captivate us with their raw beauty. These areas might seem barren at first glance, but upon closer inspection, they reveal intricate patterns formed by the wind and weather, traces of life adapted to harsh conditions, and a serene stillness that is often hard to find in our busy lives. The emptiness of these terrains allows us to appreciate the subtle details and marvel at nature's resilience and creativity. It invites us to slow down, observe, and reflect, fostering a deeper connection with the natural world.

Uncluttered spaces also play a crucial role in sparking imagination and offering opportunities for growth. In a world where we are constantly bombarded with information and stimuli, finding a space free from distractions can be incredibly liberating. These places provide a blank canvas, encouraging us to think freely and creatively without the constraints of pre-existing structures or expectations. Empty rooms, expansive fields, and even the clear blue sky can serve as stages for our minds to wander, dream, and innovate.

For example, many artists, writers, and thinkers have found inspiration in simplicity and minimalism. By stripping away the unnecessary, they create works that resonate deeply and offer new perspectives. The painter who starts with a blank canvas or the writer who faces an empty page understands the power of nothingness in fueling creativity. It is within this void that possibilities become endless, and new ideas can take shape and flourish. This concept underscores the importance of allowing ourselves time and space to unplug, declutter, and let our minds roam freely.

Recognizing the charm of nothingness challenges the traditional notion that emptiness equals lack. On the contrary, embracing nothingness can be a source of profound beauty and fulfillment. Just as silence between musical notes creates rhythm and depth, so does emptiness provide balance and contrast in our lives. It allows us to appreciate what we have, the spaces we inhabit, and the moments we experience more fully. This perspective shift can lead to a greater sense of gratitude and contentment, enriching our overall well-being.

In untouched landscapes, we find realms that invite us to dream beyond mortal boundaries and awareness.

These spaces, unaltered by human hands, represent purity and potential. They remind us of the world's natural state, unspoiled and ripe with possibilities. By immersing ourselves in such environments, we can transcend the limitations of everyday life and tap into a deeper sense of wonder and awe. These experiences can be transformative, expanding our consciousness and opening our minds to new avenues of thought and understanding.

Moreover, exploring these pristine landscapes encourages us to consider our role in preserving and protecting the natural world. It prompts us to think about how we can coexist harmoniously with our environment and ensure that future generations can also experience the magic of untouched spaces. This awareness can inspire actions that contribute to sustainable living and environmental stewardship, creating a ripple effect of positive change.

Embracing the Splendor and Potential of Nothingness

The exploration of nothingness throughout this chapter has highlighted its inherent potential and beauty, shifting our perception from one of absence to a realm brimming with possibilities. This reframed understanding invites us to appreciate the blank canvases in our lives not as empty or lacking but as opportunities for creativity, growth, and transformation.

Revisiting the initial perspective, where we examined how an empty space can be seen as a fertile ground for new ideas and dreams, we see that this concept holds significant value. Whether it's an artist staring at an empty canvas, a writer facing a blank page, or anyone encountering a moment of stillness, these experiences are characterized by their potential rather than their emptiness. They allow for experimentation, mistakes, and ultimately personal growth, devoid of pre-existing patterns that could stifle creativity.

In daily life, creating environments free from clutter and distraction can foster such moments. Simple practices like taking a walk in a quiet park or dedicating time to silent meditation help reconnect us with our inner thoughts, offering fresh perspectives and nurturing creativity. Recognizing and embracing periods of nothingness enables breakthroughs and innovations that might otherwise remain obscured by constant activity and noise.

The chapter also discussed historical and cultural viewpoints on nothingness, ranging from Eastern philosophies like Buddhism and Taoism to existentialist perspectives. These various lenses enrich our understanding, illustrating how nothingness can be a path to enlightenment, peace, or personal meaning. For instance, Buddhist concepts of Śūnyatā emphasize liberation from attachments through understanding emptiness, while existentialists like Sartre see it as a canvas for individual significance in the absence of inherent meaning.

The practice of minimalism, which emphasizes simplifying one's surroundings to amplify personal fulfillment, further exemplifies the benefits of embracing nothingness. By intentionally clearing out physical and mental clutter, individuals can focus on what truly matters, leading to greater clarity, purpose, and mastery in different areas of life.

However, some readers may find the idea of embracing nothingness unsettling, as it challenges deeply ingrained notions of productivity, accumulation, and perpetual engagement. There is a concern that in a society constantly pushing for more —more possessions, more achievements, more interactions— pausing to appreciate nothingness may feel counterintuitive or unproductive.

Yet, the broader implications suggest that integrating moments of nothingness into our lives can lead to a more balanced and fulfilling existence. It encourages a shift away from relentless consumption and toward a deeper appreciation of simplicity and tranquility.

This balance can enhance overall well-being, allowing for more meaningful and intentional living.

Ultimately, embracing nothingness invites us to view the world with fresh eyes and open minds. It is about finding beauty and potential in what appears empty and appreciating the serenity that comes with stillness. As we continue to explore and integrate these ideas, we may uncover new depths within ourselves and our surroundings, enriching our lives in ways we had not previously imagined. The journey towards understanding and harnessing nothingness is ongoing, promising continuous growth, reflection, and discovery.

CHAPTER 2
The Resonance of Silence

Silence influences various aspects of our lives, offering more than just a respite from the noise around us. In an era where constant chatter and distractions are prevalent, silence stands as a powerful tool that can deeply affect our self-awareness, personal growth, and connection to the world. Embracing moments of quiet allows us to step back from the perpetual noise and engage in meaningful reflection. It is within these pockets of serenity that one can discover profound shifts in perception, understanding, and emotional clarity.

This chapter delves into the multifaceted nature of silence and its transformative effects on our mental and emotional states. We will explore how silence fosters self-reflection, leading to increased self-awareness and personal insights. The narrative will also highlight the role of silence in enhancing problem-solving abilities and creativity by providing our minds with the space they need to process information without interruptions. Another significant aspect covered will be the restorative power of silence, which helps in reducing stress and promoting overall well-being. Finally, the chapter will discuss the broader implications of silence on our relationships and interactions, showing how it can lead to deeper connections and improved communication with others. Through these discussions, we hope to illuminate the often-overlooked resonance of silence in our daily lives.

Silence as a Transformative Presence

Silence offers a sanctuary for thoughts to crystallize and the mind to find calm. In our fast-paced world, moments of silence are rare yet profoundly impactful. It provides a refuge from constant noise, allowing the mind to settle and our thoughts to become more coherent. When we carve out moments of quietude, our brains can process information without interruptions, leading to better problem-solving skills and heightened creativity.

Moreover, silence can be deeply restorative. Without the distraction of external noise, the mind can relax and release accumulated stress. This break from auditory stimuli can result in improved mental clarity and emotional stability. Individuals often report feeling more centered and balanced after spending time in silence, which is crucial for maintaining overall well-being.

Silence also allows for reflection that can lead to insight and understanding. By tuning out the external world, we give space for our inner dialogue to emerge.
This introspective process helps us to understand ourselves better and make thoughtful decisions. In this

way, silence is not just an absence of sound but a powerful tool for personal growth and cognitive function.

Silence broadens our awareness and provides clarity amidst life's clamor. In the hustle and bustle of daily life, it's easy to overlook the finer details and lose sight of what truly matters. Silence gives us the opportunity to pause and notice these subtleties, enhancing our perception of the world around us. When we quiet our minds, we become more attuned to our surroundings and more present in our experiences.

This heightened awareness can lead to greater appreciation and gratitude for the small, often overlooked aspects of life. By focusing on moments of silence, we can cultivate a deeper sense of mindfulness and connection to the present. This awareness can extend into our relationships, improving communication and empathy with those around us.

Furthermore, clarity brought by silence enables us to prioritize our goals and values. When we remove distractions, we can focus more deeply on what is important to us. This can lead to more intentional living, where our actions align more closely with our true desires and aspirations. By regularly practicing silence, we can maintain this level of clarity and purpose.

Pursuing silence helps in introspection and grounding oneself in the present moment. Modern life often pulls us in multiple directions, making it challenging to stay present. Silence acts as a powerful anchor, bringing us back to the here and now. It encourages us to slow down, breathe, and experience each moment fully, fostering a richer and more meaningful existence.

In moments of silence, we can engage in deep introspection, examining our thoughts, feelings, and behaviors without judgment. This self-reflection is crucial for personal development, as it allows us to identify areas for growth and change. Through regular practice, silence can become a habit that nurtures continuous self-improvement and emotional resilience.

Grounding oneself in the present moment through silence also enhances our ability to cope with stress. By focusing on the present, we can reduce anxiety about the future and ruminations on the past. This mindfulness practice can lead to greater emotional stability and peace of mind, enabling us to handle life's challenges with grace and composure.

Silence acts as a crucible for self-discovery, allowing individuals to navigate thoughts and feelings more effectively. When we embrace silence, we create space for our innermost thoughts and emotions to surface.

This process can be enlightening, as it reveals aspects of ourselves that we may not have been aware of before. Through silence, we can gain a deeper understanding of our motivations, fears, and desires.

Navigating these thoughts and feelings in silence can lead to significant breakthroughs in self-awareness. We can confront unresolved issues, recognize patterns in our behavior, and develop a more authentic sense of self. This journey of self-discovery is essential for personal growth, as it equips us with the knowledge and insight needed to make positive changes in our lives.

Additionally, the practice of embracing silence can enhance our emotional intelligence. By regularly tuning into our inner landscape, we become more adept at identifying and managing our emotions. This skill is invaluable in both personal and professional settings, as it fosters better decision-making, improved relationships, and greater overall well-being.

The Depths of Introspection Through Silence

Silence frees us from external cacophony, making us more receptive to inner dialogue. In a world constantly abuzz with noise, it becomes increasingly challenging to tune into our internal landscape. The relentless stream of sounds and voices can create a barrier that distances us from our true selves. When we embrace silence, these barriers begin to dissolve. This newfound quietude allows us to focus on our thoughts and emotions, fostering deeper self-reflection.

Consider how silence at the end of a hectic day feels like a breath of fresh air. It is in these moments, away from the commotion, that our minds have the opportunity to wander freely. Suddenly, ideas that were previously obscured come to light. This clarity spurs profound realizations about our aspirations, fears, and uncertainties. Removing external distractions reveals layers of inner dialogue that often go unnoticed amidst daily chaos.

Moreover, silence doesn't merely offer a respite; it actively paves the way for self-discovery. By turning inward, we start to notice recurring themes or concerns that might warrant attention. These inner conversations could lead to powerful insights, such as recognizing suppressed emotions or understanding long-held beliefs. Silence thus becomes a crucial tool for anyone keen to uncover their innermost thoughts and navigate their mental landscape with greater awareness.

It also allows us to attend to subtle emotions, intuition, and inner wisdom. Often, the rush of daily life muffles our ability to perceive these gentle signals. It's like trying to hear a whisper in a crowded room—virtually impossible. Creating pockets of silence changes this dynamic drastically. We become attuned to the finer nuances of our emotional states, which might otherwise be drowned out by everyday noise.

Attending to subtle emotions involves recognizing fleeting feelings that may hold significant meaning. For instance, a brief moment of discomfort around a certain topic could be an indicator of unresolved issues. In silence, we can pay attention to such cues and explore them without distraction. This practice heightens our emotional intelligence, aiding in better self-regulation and a deeper understanding of what truly affects us.

Intuition and inner wisdom also thrive in silent spaces. Without constant input from external sources, our intuitive thoughts gain prominence. These are those gut feelings or sudden flashes of insight that guide decisions and offer perspectives we might not achieve through logic alone. Quiet moments allow these intuitive voices to speak louder, offering guidance that is both personal and profound. Engaging with silence regularly fine-tunes our ability to tap into this rich well of inner wisdom, enriching our decision-making processes and overall sense of direction.

We discern both vulnerabilities and strengths, enhancing self-awareness. Silence acts as a mirror, reflecting our true selves back at us. In the absence of noise, there's no escaping our authentic thoughts and feelings. This encounter with our unfiltered selves can both be revealing and transformative. We come face to face with our vulnerabilities, recognizing fears, insecurities, or unresolved emotions that need addressing. Acknowledging these aspects of ourselves is the first step toward healing and growth.

Simultaneously, silence highlights our strengths. It provides a space where we can appreciate our achievements, inherent talents, and resilience. This balanced view fosters a healthier self-image, as we learn to value our positive attributes alongside acknowledging areas for improvement. Such comprehensive self-awareness is crucial for personal development. It empowers us to leverage our strengths while working on our vulnerabilities, leading to a more fulfilled and balanced life.

Furthermore, this heightened self-awareness encourages self-compassion. When we understand our struggles and strengths, we're more likely to treat ourselves with kindness and empathy. Instead of harsh self-criticism, we begin to support and nurture our journey towards personal growth. Embracing silence thus becomes a practice of cultivating a compassionate and holistic relationship with oneself.

Engaging with silence fosters deeper connections with our authentic selves. In a noisy world often dominated by external expectations, it's easy to lose sight of who we truly are. Silence serves as a sanctuary where we can reconnect with our core values, passions, and desires. Stripped of external influences, we gain clarity about what genuinely matters to us, allowing our authentic selves to emerge.

This process of reconnection involves introspection and honest self-examination. In silence, we can question whether our current path aligns with our true aspirations or if we've strayed due to societal pressures. Such reflections enable us to make choices that are more congruent with our authentic selves, leading to a more satisfying and meaningful life. By regularly engaging in silence, we maintain this alignment, continually steering our lives in a direction that resonates with our deepest convictions.

In addition, connecting with our authentic selves through silence enhances our interactions with others. When we understand and accept who we are, we engage more authentically with those around us. This authenticity fosters genuine relationships based on mutual respect and understanding. As we present our true selves to the world, we invite others to do the same, creating a ripple effect that promotes deeper, more meaningful connections. Thus, silence not only nurtures our inner life but also enriches our external relationships, affirming that our pursuit of quietude has far-reaching benefits.

Clarity and Robust Presence through Silence

Silence is an often underappreciated yet immensely powerful tool in our lives. Undisturbed silence offers a sanctuary from the relentless whirlwind of daily noise, allowing our minds to settle and achieve greater clarity. In moments of stillness, the mental fog that often clouds our thoughts dissipates, providing a clearer perspective. This newfound mental clarity enables us to process information more effectively, think more deeply, and understand situations with greater acuity.

When we embrace silence, we can discern complex situations with remarkable precision. Without the distractions of external noise, our cognitive functions sharpen, enhancing our ability to evaluate circumstances and make informed decisions. This heightened level of discernment allows us to see beyond the superficial, understanding the essence of issues that might otherwise elude us. By honing this skill through regular periods of undisturbed silence, we develop a truer sense of judgment.

The absence of constant noise grounds individuals firmly in the present moment. This grounding effect pulls our attention away from past regrets and future anxieties, anchoring us in the now. As we focus on the current moment, our minds become less cluttered, and our ability to concentrate improves. This enhanced focus can lead to increased productivity and a more profound appreciation for life's subtleties.

A clarified mind is a powerful asset for anyone seeking purpose and direction. When mental clutter is cleared, our core values and true intentions come into sharper focus. We begin to identify what genuinely matters to us, aligning our actions and decisions with our authentic selves. This alignment fosters a strong sense of purpose, guiding us through life with confidence and conviction.

Freed from the cacophony outside, we become more receptive to our innermost dialogue. The quiet moments allow us to listen to our hearts' subtle murmurs and the nudges of our intuition. Engaging with these internal voices helps us navigate our thoughts and feelings with heightened awareness. This inward focus cultivates self-awareness, enabling us to understand our motivations and emotions more thoroughly.

Silence's Connection to Personal Growth

Venturing into silence is akin to entering a realm of healing and evolution. When we consciously choose to embrace silence, we often find ourselves on a path toward inner peace and self-discovery. This quiet time allows the mind to rest and rejuvenate, breaking away from the constant stream of information and noise that floods our daily lives. Through this withdrawal from external chaos, our internal healing processes are activated, promoting mental clarity and emotional balance.

In this serene state, our minds are free to explore deeper thoughts and emotions that often go unnoticed in the rush of everyday life. It becomes a period of profound introspection where unresolved issues can surface and be addressed. By confronting these hidden aspects of ourselves, we begin a journey of personal growth that fosters resilience and emotional well-being. Silence, in essence, becomes a fertile ground for psychological repair and development.

Moreover, as we continue to embrace silence, we notice gradual but significant changes in our overall wellness. The reduction of stress and anxiety not only improves mental health but also has positive effects on physical health. Lower blood pressure, better sleep, and improved immune function are just some of the benefits linked to periods of quiet reflection. Thus, silence not only heals the mind but also fortifies the body, paving the way for a more holistic approach to wellness.

Silence bridges connections to inner wisdom and unveils fresh perspectives. In the absence of external distractions, we become more attuned to our inner voice—our intuition. This heightened awareness fosters a stronger connection with our deepest values and beliefs. By listening more intently to our inner guidance, we can make decisions that align more closely with our true selves, leading to greater satisfaction and meaning in life.

This deepened connection to inner wisdom also sparks new ways of seeing the world around us. When the mind is calm and uncluttered, it is more capable of generating innovative solutions to problems and recognizing opportunities that may have been previously overlooked. Fresh perspectives emerge as we develop a more nuanced understanding of our experiences and surroundings. These insights can lead to personal transformation and a renewed sense of purpose.

Furthermore, by regularly practicing silence, we cultivate a habit of mindfulness that enriches our daily existence. Mindfulness encourages us to fully engage with each moment, enhancing our appreciation for the simple joys of life. As our awareness expands, we become more present and attentive, fostering a deeper connection not just with ourselves but also with others. This mindful presence nurtures empathy and compassion, reinforcing the bonds that tie us to our communities and the world at large.

Silence enhances creativity, inspiration, and personal tenacity. When we allow our minds to bask in stillness, we create space for creativity to flourish.
Without the constant barrage of stimuli, our brains can wander freely, making novel connections and generating original ideas. This creative freedom imparts a sense of joy and fulfillment, as we tap into our innate potential to innovate and express ourselves.

Inspiration often follows naturally from this wellspring of creativity. Moments of silence can serve as powerful catalysts for epiphanies and breakthroughs. Many great thinkers and artists have attributed their most profound insights to periods of quiet contemplation. By integrating silence into our routines, we offer ourselves the opportunity to access this unbounded source of inspiration, propelling us forward in our personal and professional endeavors.

Building on this foundation of creativity and inspiration is personal tenacity—the inner strength to pursue our goals despite challenges. Silence enables us to reflect on our aspirations and reaffirm our commitment to them.

This introspective focus strengthens our resolve, helping us to push through obstacles with determination and persistence. In this way, silence becomes a crucial ally in our pursuit of success and self-actualization.

It strengthens empathy, compassion, and comprehension, fostering a deeper bond with the world. Spending time in silence sharpens our ability to empathize with others. By turning inward and reflecting on our own experiences and emotions, we gain a better understanding of what others might be going through. This enhanced empathy allows us to connect more genuinely with those around us, building stronger and more meaningful relationships.

In addition to empathy, silence nurtures compassion. As we become more aware of our vulnerabilities and strengths, we develop a kinder and more forgiving attitude towards ourselves. This self-compassion naturally extends to others, encouraging us to act with greater kindness and consideration. Our interactions become more supportive and nurturing, creating an environment where everyone can thrive.

Finally, silence promotes deeper comprehension of complex situations and interpersonal dynamics. With a clear and focused mind, we are better equipped to listen actively, not passively, to see and understand different perspectives. This increased comprehension helps us navigate social interactions more effectively, reducing misunderstandings and conflicts. By fostering open and empathetic communication, silence strengthens our connections with others and enhances our collective well-being.

Silence in Communication and Relationships

Silence can be a versatile tool in communication. Used positively, it has the potential to create a space for reflection and deeper understanding between individuals. Silence allows us to pause, breathe, and fully absorb what has been communicated before responding thoughtfully. It provides an opportunity to gather one's thoughts and articulate responses in a more measured and meaningful way. Effective use of silence can lead to more honest and thoughtful exchanges, strengthening the overall quality of communication.

Conversely, silence can also serve a negative role in conversations. For instance, when used to withdraw emotionally or evade difficult topics, it can create confusion and anxiety. This type of silence can leave the other party feeling neglected or misunderstood. The absence of verbal interaction might be misinterpreted as disengagement or disinterest, potentially causing a rift in the relationship. Understanding the intention behind the silence is crucial in these scenarios to avoid miscommunication.

It is important to note that the impact of silence is not universal and can vary significantly based on context. In some cultures, silence is valued and seen as a sign of respect or wisdom. In others, it may be perceived as awkward or even rude. Recognizing these cultural differences helps in navigating interpersonal interactions more effectively. For instance, in high-context cultures like Japan, silence often carries significant weight and meaning, serving as a powerful communicative tool.

Silence in communication can indicate emotional withdrawal or affirm true listening and understanding. When someone chooses to remain silent during a conversation, it may suggest that they are processing emotions internally. Emotional withdrawal through silence can be a coping mechanism, but if prolonged, it may isolate the individual further. Therefore, recognizing and addressing emotional withdrawal is essential to maintaining healthy communication.

On the other hand, silence can also signify deep engagement and empathy. When someone listens without interruption, it shows that they value the speaker's words and are fully present in the moment. This form of active listening can validate the speaker's feelings and experiences, fostering a sense of trust and connection. Such moments of shared silence can be incredibly powerful, allowing both parties to connect on a deeper level.

Different cultural contexts significantly influence how silence is interpreted and used in communication. In some Western societies, where verbal expression is highly valued, silence might be seen as uncomfortable or indicative of a lack of interest. Conversely, many Eastern cultures place a higher value on non-verbal communication, where silence is considered a critical component of respectful dialogue.

Understanding these cultural nuances is vital in international or multicultural interactions. Misinterpretations of silence can lead to misunderstandings or even conflict. Being aware of and sensitive to these cultural differences can enhance communication and foster more positive relationships. For instance, recognizing that silence in certain cultures signifies contemplation rather than disinterest can prevent unnecessary tension and promote mutual respect.

Appropriate use of silence in communication can enhance relationship dynamics. Knowing when to speak and when to remain silent demonstrates emotional intelligence and respect for the other person's needs and boundaries. For example, offering silent support during a friend's moment of grief can be more comforting than trying to fill the void with words. It demonstrates empathy and acknowledges that sometimes, silence speaks louder than words.

In professional settings, strategic use of silence can also play a pivotal role. During negotiations, pausing to think before responding can convey confidence and thoughtfulness, potentially leading to better outcomes. Silence can also be a powerful tool in leadership, where giving team members space to voice their ideas uninterrupted can foster innovation and collaboration.

Physical and Psychological Benefits of Silence

Spending time in silence can significantly reduce blood pressure and cortisol levels, which is pivotal for overall health. Numerous studies have shown that periods of quietude can lead to decreased blood pressure, a major indicator of cardiovascular health. When we immerse ourselves in silence, our bodies shift into a state of relaxation that allows for the dilation of blood vessels, leading to improved blood flow and lower blood pressure. This physiological response helps mitigate the long-term risks associated with hypertension, such as heart disease and stroke.

Cortisol, often referred to as the "stress hormone," is released during times of stress and has various effects on the body. Prolonged elevated levels of cortisol can lead to numerous health issues, including anxiety, depression, and impaired cognitive performance. Engaging in regular silent practices can effectively reduce cortisol levels, thereby diminishing its adverse impacts. This reduction fosters a calmer mental state and improves one's ability to manage stress and anxiety, contributing to better mental and emotional well-being.

These health benefits of reduced blood pressure and cortisol are further supported by research from medical institutions and many psychological studies.

Ensuring a routine that involves moments of silence, whether through meditation, mindfulness, or simply sitting quietly, can be an accessible strategy to improve these aspects of physical health. Integrating silence into daily life thus becomes not just a personal choice but a healthful practice with tangible benefits.

Silence also plays a critical role in promoting hormone regulation. Hormones act as chemical messengers in the body and are essential for regulating various physiological processes. Spending time in silence can help balance hormone levels, supporting functions like metabolism, immune response, and reproductive health. For example, silence has been linked to increased production of endorphins and serotonin, hormones associated with mood regulation and feelings of well-being.

Moreover, silence can prevent arterial plaque formation, thereby protecting against atherosclerosis — a condition characterized by the build-up of plaques in the arteries. This build-up can lead to serious cardiovascular diseases, such as heart attacks and strokes. By reducing stress and promoting a relaxed state, silence indirectly supports healthier arteries and minimizes plaque accumulation. This protective mechanism highlights the importance of silence in maintaining cardiac health.

The interaction between silence and hormone regulation extends to enhancing sleep quality. Balanced hormones, particularly melatonin, are crucial for restoring healthy sleep patterns, and silence before bedtime can create an optimal environment for melatonin production. Improved sleep, in turn, supports overall health, proving how silence weaves itself into the tapestry of our well-being.

Silence is also a fertile ground for enhancing creativity, focus, self-control, and self-awareness. In a world bombarded with constant stimuli, finding moments of silence allows the mind to wander and explore new ideas. Creativity flourishes when the mind is free from external distractions, offering space for novel thoughts and solutions to emerge. This creative boost is invaluable for problem-solving and artistic endeavors alike.

Focus is another area impacted by silence. By eliminating background noise and interruptions, silence provides a conducive environment for deep concentration. This heightened focus facilitates productivity and the execution of tasks with greater precision. The ability to concentrate deeply is crucial in both professional and personal settings, enabling individuals to perform more efficiently and effectively.

Self-control and self-awareness are intertwined qualities that are nurtured through silence. When external chatter is minimized, individuals can turn their attention inward, gaining clarity on their thoughts, emotions, and behaviors. This introspection leads to a better understanding of oneself, fostering a sense of control over impulses and reactions. As self-awareness increases, so does the ability to make conscious choices aligned with personal values and goals.

Finally, cultivating a deeper sense of perspective and spirituality is one of the most profound benefits of spending time in silence. Silence invites contemplation and introspection, allowing individuals to reflect on their lives and place within the universe. This reflection can lead to a broader perspective, helping to put everyday challenges into context and fostering a sense of gratitude and contentment.

Spirituality often finds a natural companion in silence. Many spiritual traditions emphasize the importance of silence for connecting with the divine or the inner self. Moments of stillness can be a gateway to experiencing a deeper, transcendent reality, fostering a sense of unity with something greater than oneself. This spiritual connection can provide comfort, guidance, and a profound sense of peace.

The Power and Potential Variability of Silence

Throughout this chapter, we have explored the transformative power of silence and its impact on self-awareness, personal growth, and our connection with the world. By delving into how silence offers a refuge from constant noise, we have seen how it allows the mind to settle, leading to better problem-solving skills and heightened creativity. The restorative qualities of silence have also been highlighted, showing how it helps release accumulated stress and enhances emotional stability.

Returning to our initial statement about the significance of silence, it's evident that carving out these moments of quietude provides an invaluable opportunity for introspection and grounding oneself in the present moment. Silence acts as an anchor, enabling us to slow down, breathe, and fully experience each moment. This practice not only fosters a richer existence but also enhances our ability to cope with stress, leading to greater emotional resilience and peace of mind.

As we consider our current position, it becomes clear that regular engagement with silence can lead to significant breakthroughs in self-awareness and personal development. Embracing silence allows us to navigate our thoughts and feelings more effectively, uncovering motivations, fears, and desires that might have remained hidden amidst daily chaos. This deeper understanding of ourselves equips us with the knowledge needed to make positive changes in our lives, enhancing both emotional intelligence and decision-making.

However, some readers may be concerned about the practical aspects of incorporating silence into their busy lives. Modern life is often characterized by constant activity and distractions, making it challenging to find uninterrupted quiet time. Yet, even short periods of silence can be immensely beneficial. Simple practices like mindful breathing, taking a few minutes of silence before starting the day, or creating a quiet space at home can pave the way for significant mental and emotional benefits.

On a wider scale, the consequences of embracing silence are far-reaching. As individuals cultivate a habit of introspection and mindfulness, there is potential for a collective shift towards greater empathy, compassion, and understanding in our communities. Improved self-awareness can enhance communication and relationships, fostering a more connected and harmonious society. Additionally, the mental and physical health benefits associated with silence can contribute to overall well-being, reducing stress-related ailments and promoting a healthier lifestyle.

In conclusion, the journey through silence is an ongoing process of discovery and growth. It allows us to reconnect with our authentic selves, align our actions with our true aspirations, and navigate life's challenges with clarity and composure. As we continue to explore and embrace the depths of silence, we open ourselves to a deeper connection with the world around us and the boundless potential within.

CHAPTER 3
The Power of Letting Go

Letting go is a transformative process that can pave the way for greater personal liberation and growth. It involves a conscious decision to release what no longer serves us, be it material possessions, outdated beliefs, or unproductive relationships. This very act of relinquishing opens up new avenues for self-discovery and mindfulness, allowing us to reconnect with our inner selves in more meaningful ways. By understanding and practicing the art of letting go, we create space for clarity, peace, and fresh opportunities that align with our core values and aspirations.

This chapter delves into the multifaceted nature of decluttering and its impact on our mental and emotional well-being. It explores how reducing both physical and mental clutter can lead to enhanced focus and serenity. The discussion extends to strategies for identifying non-essential items, commitments, and belief systems that may hinder personal progress. Readers will gain insights into how letting go can foster mindfulness, improve productivity, and cultivate a renewed sense of purpose. Through practical examples and reflective practices, this chapter aims to equip individuals with the tools to navigate the complexities of their lives and embrace change as a natural part of their growth journey.

Understanding the Art of Decluttering

Decluttering our lives from the non-essential is an important practice that can have profound effects on our well-being and personal growth. In a world where we are constantly bombarded with stimuli, possessions, and obligations, finding the space to breathe and reflect becomes crucial. This act of decluttering isn't just about physical spaces but also encompasses mental and emotional facets of our lives. When we intentionally remove what doesn't serve us, we allow ourselves to experience a serene simplicity and focus that is often missing in modern life.

Emphasizing how decluttering reveals the serene beauty of emptiness is a key aspect of this practice. When we strip away the excess, we begin to see the inherent beauty in simplicity. Our surroundings become less cluttered, creating a peaceful environment that fosters calmness and clarity. Emotionally, letting go of unnecessary burdens provides a sense of relief and liberation, allowing us to connect more deeply with our true selves. The spaciousness that comes from decluttering opens up room for new opportunities and experiences, enriching our lives in unexpected ways.

Furthermore, the act of decluttering can be seen as a path to mindfulness. By consciously choosing what to keep and what to discard, we engage in a process of self-reflection. This allows us to evaluate our priorities and make decisions that align with our values. The newfound clarity we gain helps us navigate life with greater intention and purpose, leading to a more fulfilling existence.

Modern life's distractions make the practice of decluttering necessary. With the advent of technology and the constant influx of information, our attention is perpetually divided. Social media, emails, advertisements, and news updates compete for our focus, leaving us overwhelmed and mentally exhausted. These distractions not only clutter our minds but also prevent us from being fully present in our daily lives. By reducing these distractions, we create the mental space needed to concentrate on what truly matters.

In addition to digital distractions, physical clutter in our living and working spaces can contribute to stress and anxiety. A cluttered environment often leads to a cluttered mind, making it difficult to think clearly and make decisions. Tidying up our spaces can have a calming effect, promoting a sense of order and control. As we declutter our physical surroundings, we simultaneously declutter our minds, paving the way for enhanced productivity and creativity.

Mental clutter, such as incessant worry and negative thought patterns, also demands attention. Practicing mindfulness techniques, such as meditation and journaling, can help clear this mental clutter. By dedicating time to quiet reflection, we train our minds to let go of unproductive thoughts and focus on the present moment. In doing so, we cultivate a sense of inner peace and resilience, better equipped to handle life's challenges.

Exploring specific examples of what constitutes 'nonessential' in our lives can provide practical insights into the decluttering process. Non-essential items vary from person to person, but common examples include material possessions that no longer serve a purpose or bring joy. Clothes that haven't been worn in years, outdated gadgets, and redundant home decor are all candidates for removal. By assessing each item's value and utility, we can make informed decisions about what to keep and what to let go.

Beyond physical items, reevaluating our commitments and relationships is equally important. Obligations that drain our energy without adding value to our lives should be reconsidered. This might involve setting boundaries, saying no more often, or distancing ourselves from toxic relationships. Letting go of such commitments frees up time and energy for pursuits that align with our goals and passions.

Additionally, identifying and eliminating limiting beliefs and behaviors is a crucial aspect of decluttering. These internal barriers can prevent us from realizing our full potential. By challenging and reframing these beliefs, we open ourselves up to new possibilities and growth. For instance, overcoming the fear of failure can enable us to take risks and embrace opportunities that lead to personal and professional development.

The benefits of decluttering extend beyond the immediate relief of removing excess; they include long-term advantages such as mental clarity and focused living. When we clear out the non-essential, we uncover the essentials—what truly matters to us. This newfound clarity enables us to set meaningful goals and pursue them with unwavering focus. With fewer distractions, our decision-making improves, and we become more efficient in our daily tasks.

Moreover, a decluttered life promotes mental well-being. The sense of accomplishment that comes from organizing our spaces and minds can boost our confidence and reduce feelings of overwhelm. It creates an environment where we feel more in control, fostering a positive mindset. This mental clarity allows us to approach challenges with a calm and composed demeanor, enhancing our problem-solving abilities.

Standing Against Societal Pressures

In today's world, we are constantly bombarded by a relentless digital and information overload. Every glance at our phones or computers inundates us with an array of notifications, updates, and messages. This ceaseless flow of information creates an environment where introspection and genuine self-reflection become rare commodities. We find ourselves perpetually engaged in superficial interactions and consumption of content, leaving little room for deeper thoughts and connections. The sheer volume of data can overwhelm our minds, making it challenging to discern what is truly meaningful.

Amidst this whirlwind, letting go shines as a beacon to help us achieve a more rewarding practice of mindfulness and focus on our true selves. By consciously choosing to disconnect from the constant barrage of information, we allow space for introspection and personal growth. This act of letting go is not about rejecting technology outright but rather about setting boundaries that enable us to reclaim control over our mental landscape. It involves being selective about the information we consume and prioritizing quality over quantity.

Moreover, letting go of the need to always stay updated liberates us from the anxiety of missing out. It encourages us to be present in the moment and engage with the world around us authentically. In doing so, we begin to appreciate the simplicity and depth of real-life interactions and experiences. Letting go thus becomes a powerful tool in countering the pervasive influence of digital and information overload, helping us to reconnect with our inner selves and find balance in an overstimulated world.

Societal norms exert significant pressure on individuals to conform to certain roles and expectations. From a young age, we are taught to follow predefined paths that often prioritize external validation over personal fulfillment. These norms dictate how we should behave, what careers we should pursue, and even how we should interact with others. The pressure to conform can stifle creativity and hinder the pursuit of one's true passions. One of the most profound steps in this journey is letting go of societal expectations. By doing so, we begin to question and redefine the metrics of success and happiness. We start to recognize that true fulfillment comes from aligning our actions with our core values and aspirations rather than blindly adhering to societal dictates. Letting go of these external pressures allows us to explore unconventional paths, embrace our uniqueness, and make choices that resonate with our authentic selves.

Furthermore, letting go empowers us to resist the urge to compare ourselves with others constantly. It alleviates the burden of feeling inadequate based on societal standards, fostering a healthier self-image and greater self-acceptance. Embracing our individuality and rejecting the pressure to fit into prescribed molds fosters a sense of liberation and opens up new possibilities for personal growth and happiness.

The internal conflict between societal expectations and individual aspirations can create significant stress and dissatisfaction. On one hand, there is an innate desire to fulfill one's potential and pursue personal dreams.

On the other hand, there is a fear of deviating from accepted norms and facing potential judgment or failure. This tug-of-war can lead to a life filled with compromises and unfulfilled desires, ultimately hampering personal growth.

Addressing this internal conflict requires a conscious effort to prioritize personal aspirations over societal expectations. It involves introspection and self-awareness to understand what truly matters to us beyond external validation. Letting go of the need to meet every societal expectation frees us to focus on what brings genuine joy and meaning to our lives. It is a courageous step towards self-liberation and living authentically.

By resolving this internal conflict, we pave the way for a more harmonious and fulfilling existence. We learn to trust our instincts and decisions, cultivating a sense of confidence and self-assurance. This shift in mindset transforms our approach to life, allowing us to pursue our passions wholeheartedly and without reservation. In essence, letting go of societal expectations and embracing personal aspirations leads to a more profound sense of satisfaction and well-being.

Prioritizing personal dreams over societal demands is a liberating experience that fosters remarkable personal growth. Society often imposes a rigid framework of what is considered successful or acceptable, which may not align with our individual goals and ambitions.

Breaking free from these chains enables us to chart our courses and live life on our terms.

Choosing to prioritize personal dreams involves a radical shift in perspective. It means valuing our intrinsic motivations and desires above the expectations imposed by others. This transition may involve making difficult choices, such as changing careers, relocating, or adopting unconventional lifestyles. However, the rewards of pursuing our dreams far outweigh the temporary discomforts.

Navigating Personal Attachments and Beliefs

Attachments manifest in many forms. Whether it's relationships with people, ownership of material possessions, or even personal beliefs and self-identities, these attachments can significantly influence our lives. Relationships can be deeply fulfilling but also challenging when dependence grows. We might cling to these connections out of fear, nostalgia, or a sense of obligation, often at the expense of our well-being. Material possessions, on the other hand, may provide comfort or status but can also weigh us down with their maintenance and the constant desire for more.

Similarly, our beliefs and self-identities are powerful forces shaping our actions and decisions. Over time, some of these core beliefs may become outdated, no longer serving our growth or happiness. Holding onto them can create a sense of stagnation. For instance, adhering to an old career identity despite an evolving passion elsewhere may confine someone to a life of unfulfillment. In recognizing these various forms of attachment, we start the journey towards evaluating their true impact on our lives.

The emotional burden of holding onto these attachments is often underestimated. They can create unseen limitations that hinder our ability to experience life fully. Emotional turbulence, such as anxiety or depression, can stem from clinging to unhealthy relationships. The weight of material possessions can lead to stress, as maintaining and safeguarding them becomes overwhelming. Even outdated beliefs can cause inner conflict, making it challenging to adapt to new experiences or perspectives.

Our minds and hearts are cluttered with the ongoing tension between maintaining these attachments and our inherent desire for change and freedom. This creates a constant state of unrest. Releasing these burdens allows an individual to take control of their emotional landscape. By letting go of what no longer serves us, we free up mental and emotional space for new, positive experiences and relationships that align better with our true selves.

Shedding old layers leads to profound renewal and rebirth. Just as trees shed their leaves to make way for new growth, individuals can experience rejuvenation by relinquishing outdated aspects of their lives. This process brings clarity and lightness, much like a fresh breeze through an open window. The newfound space invites creativity, exploration, and genuine connections, fostering a sense of liberation and empowerment.

The transformation is often marked by an increased self-awareness and authenticity. No longer tethered by past identities or possessions, people can explore their true passions and interests without restriction. This exploration encourages personal growth, allowing for the discovery of previously hidden potentials. As a result, individuals find themselves more aligned with their life's purpose and more resilient in facing future challenges.

To embark on this transformative journey, one must critically evaluate which beliefs and identities still serve their current and future well-being. Begin by reflecting on your core values and how they align with your present circumstances. Are your relationships nurturing, or do they drain your energy? Do your possessions contribute to your happiness, or do they cause stress? Are your long-held beliefs facilitating growth, or are they hindering progress?

Engage in practices such as journaling or meditation to gain deeper insights into your inner world. These reflections can help identify elements within your life that require reevaluation. It's crucial to approach this process with honesty and compassion, understanding that change is a natural part of growth. Developing a mindset oriented towards continuous reassessment helps cultivate resilience and flexibility, essential traits for navigating life's uncertainties.

Building emotional resilience is another critical strategy for managing pressure from external sources. Emotional resilience involves developing the capacity to recover quickly from difficulties and adapt to new situations positively. Practices like mindfulness, connecting with nature, and maintaining a support network can fortify one's emotional strength. By reinforcing internal stability, individuals become less susceptible to the detrimental effects of societal expectations and pressures.

Moreover, nurturing emotional resilience empowers individuals to face the inevitable periods of discomfort that accompany letting go. Recognizing the lifelong journey of adaptation and self-discovery fosters a patient and forgiving attitude towards oneself. This resilience provides the foundation for continual growth, ensuring that each release, rather than being a source of loss, becomes an opportunity for gaining something more meaningful and aligned with one's deepest aspirations.

Cultivating Emotional Resilience and Adaptability

Understanding the transient nature of life is fundamental in embracing change. Life is an ever-evolving tapestry of experiences, emotions, and phases. Nothing remains static; everything is subject to transformation, growth, and decay. Recognizing this inherent impermanence allows us to adapt more fluidly to change. It helps mitigate the fear often associated with the unknown, positioning us to approach each new development with openness rather than resistance.

One profound benefit of this understanding is a marked increase in emotional resilience. By internalizing the concept that "this too shall pass," we arm ourselves with a powerful tool to withstand life's inevitable ups and downs. This mindset fosters a perspective where challenges are seen not as insurmountable obstacles but as temporary phases. When you accept that change is a constant, you become better equipped to handle the shifts that come your way, fortifying your emotional strength.

Adapting to change doesn't just help us survive; it enables us to thrive. Each change we face carries with it unique opportunities for growth and learning. While holding on too tightly to the past can stifle progress, letting go allows us to evolve. The ability to pivot and adjust according to life's twists and turns cultivates a dynamic personal growth journey, leading to richer, more diverse experiences.

Embracing life's flux brings about a deep sense of inner peace and mental stability. When we resist change, we often experience stress and anxiety. However, by accepting that life is inherently fluid and unpredictable, we relinquish the need for control. This surrender is not about giving up but about trusting the process and allowing life to unfold naturally—a perspective that nurtures calmness and reduces tension.

Learning to float along with life's flux improves inner peace. This means acknowledging that change is not a disruption but a natural progression. As we release our grip on trying to control every outcome, we find serenity in the flow of life. This acceptance helps us remain centered and balanced, even amid chaos, fostering a stable mental and emotional state.

Moreover, this mental stability unlocks a deeper understanding of oneself and the world around us. It encourages mindfulness and living in the present moment. Rather than worrying about what could be or lamenting what has been, we focus on the now. This practice of presence enhances our overall well-being, contributing to a more peaceful and fulfilling life.

Releasing old attachments and welcoming change opens doors to new opportunities and possibilities. Every time we let go of something—be it a belief, relationship, or habit—we make space for something new to enter our lives. This cycle of release and renewal is vital for personal evolution. Holding on to outdated or unproductive aspects of our lives can block us from experiencing fresh and exciting opportunities.

This principle is evident in various aspects of life, from career changes to personal relationships. For example, leaving a stagnant job can lead to discovering a passion-driven career. Similarly, ending a toxic relationship can pave the way for healthier, more fulfilling connections. Every release, though initially daunting, creates a vacuum that attracts growth and innovation.

Loosening control and surrendering to life's organic flow is essential in this process. By relinquishing our desire to micromanage every aspect of our existence, we allow for natural growth and unexpected opportunities. Trusting that each release will bring something beneficial helps us embrace change without fear. This trust is not blind faith but a confident awareness that life tends to balance itself out in remarkable ways.

Encouraging trust and introspection are invaluable tools for overcoming vulnerabilities and fostering growth. Trust in oneself and the process of life provides a solid foundation to navigate uncertainties. Introspection, on the other hand, involves a deep self-examination to understand one's fears, desires, and motivations. Both practices are crucial in developing emotional resilience and adapting to change.

Trusting oneself requires courage and confidence. It means believing in one's capabilities to handle whatever comes their way. This trust is built through experience and self-awareness, reinforcing the idea that every challenge is an opportunity to learn and grow. As we cultivate this inner trust, we become less reliant on external validations and more secure in our path.

Introspection aids this journey by providing clarity and insight into our true selves. Regularly reflecting on our thoughts, actions, and feelings helps us identify patterns that may be holding us back. This self-awareness enables us to make conscious decisions that align with our values and goals.

Through introspection, we uncover vulnerabilities that need addressing and strengths that can bolster our resilience.

Letting go is a journey towardfreedom, authenticity, andtransformation. It involves shedding urdensomeattachments, resisting societal pressures, and embracingchange, ultimately leading to aricher and more fulfilling life.

Throughout this chapter, we have explored the transformative power of letting go and how it can lead to significant personal growth and self-liberation. The journey began with understanding the importance of decluttering not only our physical spaces but also our mental and emotional landscapes. By removing what no longer serves us, we open the door to a serene simplicity that allows for greater focus and clarity in our daily lives.

We delved into the myriad benefits of decluttering, from creating peaceful environments to fostering emotional relief and liberation. This process is not merely about tidying up; it's an act of mindfulness that helps us evaluate our priorities and align our actions with our core values. In a world filled with distractions, both digital and physical, reducing clutter becomes essential for mental well-being and productivity.

Moreover, we examined the societal pressures that often dictate our actions and decisions. From early on, many of us are conditioned to seek external validation, adhere to societal norms, and compare ourselves to others. Letting go of these pressures is crucial for achieving a more authentic and fulfilling life. It involves questioning and redefining success and happiness based on personal aspirations rather than societal expectations.

Addressing personal attachments and beliefs was another critical aspect discussed. We explored how relationships, material possessions, and outdated beliefs can weigh us down. These attachments create unseen limitations, causing emotional turbulence and hindering our ability to experience life fully. Releasing these burdens allows us to reclaim control over our emotional landscape, making space for new, positive experiences and relationships aligned with our true selves.

This chapter emphasized the importance of self-awareness and continuous reassessment in navigating personal attachments. Engaging in practices such as journaling and meditation can provide deeper insights into our inner world, helping us identify elements that require reevaluation. Embracing change as a natural part of growth fosters resilience and flexibility, essential traits for navigating life's uncertainties.

Building emotional resilience and adaptability emerged as a central theme. Understanding the transient nature of life allows us to adapt more fluidly to changes, mitigating the fear associated with the unknown. This mindset fosters emotional resilience, helping us view challenges as temporary phases rather than insurmountable obstacles. Embracing change enables us to thrive, transforming our approach to life and leading to richer, more diverse experiences.

Furthermore, we discussed the importance of releasing old attachments to welcome new opportunities. Each release creates space for growth and innovation, whether in careers, relationships, or other aspects of life. Trusting the process and loosening control over every outcome allows for natural growth, enriching our lives in unexpected ways.

As we conclude this chapter, it is evident that mastering the art of letting go is a powerful tool for self-liberation and personal growth. However, it is also a continuous journey requiring introspection, courage, and a willingness to embrace change. Readers should consider how their current attachments, beliefs, and societal pressures impact their lives and whether they align with their true values and aspirations.

On a broader scale, the practice of letting go can lead to a more mindful and present society, where individuals prioritize personal fulfillment over external validation. This shift can foster a culture of authenticity and self-acceptance, encouraging others to pursue their passions and live more meaningful lives.

Ultimately, letting go is not about loss but about creating space for what truly matters. It is an invitation to rediscover oneself, align with one's deepest values, and embrace the endless possibilities that life has to offer. As you move forward, consider what you can let go of today to make room for a brighter, more fulfilling tomorrow.

CHAPTER 4
The Dance of Dualities

Exploring the concept of duality in life reveals a profound layer of understanding about our existence. Duality, the idea that each element has its opposite, influences our perceptions and reactions to various situations. The interplay between opposites shapes our thoughts, emotions, and behaviors, impacting everything from mental health to decision-making. As we navigate through life, recognizing these dualities helps us to comprehend the nuanced nature of human experiences, enabling us to approach life's ups and downs with greater resilience and equanimity.

In this chapter, readers will delve into the multifaceted role of duality, discovering how it affects mental health by offering balanced perspectives on external opinions. The discussion extends to decision-making processes, emphasizing the importance of understanding life's spectrums to make informed choices. Furthermore, the chapter explores how duality manifests in literature and philosophy, providing insights from prominent thinkers like Camus and Nietzsche. Through these explorations, readers will gain a deeper appreciation for the inevitable contradictions in life and learn how embracing them can lead to personal growth, emotional stability, and a more fulfilling existence.

The Role of Duality in Mental Health

Understanding the concept of duality can profoundly impact mental health by reducing sensitivity to others' opinions. Duality teaches us that every opinion has its counterpart; what one person perceives as positive, another might see as negative. By grasping this simple yet powerful notion, we cultivate the ability to view criticisms and praises through a balanced lens. This awareness diminishes the emotional weight we place on others' views, allowing us to maintain our sense of self without being swayed by external judgments.

Imagine a scenario where you receive both applause and criticism for the same action. Without understanding duality, you might internalize the praise, leading to inflated self-esteem, but also be crushed by the criticism, spiraling into self-doubt. Comprehending duality offers a buffer against these extremes. It helps us realize that each opinion is just one side of the coin, neither wholly defining nor diminishing us. This realization fosters a stable emotional state, free from the turbulent swings caused by seeking validation from others.

Additionally, comprehending duality alleviates the fear of negative feedback. Knowing that opinions are inherently dual means understanding that negative perspectives are not necessarily more valid than positive ones. This clarity empowers us to navigate social interactions with confidence, acknowledging that external viewpoints do not dictate our worth. By embracing this balanced perspective, we enable ourselves to interact more genuinely, fostering healthier relationships and improved mental well-being.

Awareness of duality also plays a crucial role in maintaining emotional equilibrium. Life is replete with moments of triumphs and setbacks, and duality helps us avoid falling into the extremes of pride or self-pity. When we recognize that success and failure are two sides of the same coin, we can accept both with grace. This balance aids in preventing the ego's inflation during high points and protects against overwhelming despair during lows.

Consider the case of a professional athlete who experiences victory in one season and defeat in the next. Without the comprehension of duality, these contrasting events could lead to an oscillating emotional state, fluctuating between arrogance and dejection. However, an understanding of duality encourages the athlete to view achievements and failures as integral parts of their journey. This mindset ensures they remain grounded during successes and resilient during challenges, contributing to overall emotional stability.

Furthermore, maintaining an emotionally balanced state has physical health benefits. Stress, often exacerbated by extreme emotional reactions, can take a toll on the body. By fostering a balanced outlook through the understanding of duality, we reduce stress levels and promote a sense of calm. This holistic approach nurtures not only mental health but also supports physical well-being, leading to a healthier, more fulfilling life.

A balanced perspective derived from understanding duality also contributes significantly to the health of the body, mind, and soul. Embracing duality means accepting that life encompasses both positive and negative experiences, and this acceptance cultivates inner harmony. When we experience harmony within ourselves, it reflects positively on our physical health, mental clarity, and spiritual growth.

For instance, someone dealing with chronic illness can benefit immensely from a dualistic perspective. By recognizing that their condition brings both challenges and opportunities for personal growth, they can navigate their journey with a balanced mindset. This approach reduces the psychological burden of illness, encouraging proactive health management and enhancing quality of life. Emotional equilibrium achieved through this understanding can foster resilience, aiding in the healing process and promoting overall wellness.

Moreover, a balanced perspective nurtures a mindful approach to life's experiences. Mindfulness involves being present and accepting each moment as it is, without excessive attachment or aversion. Understanding duality aligns perfectly with mindfulness, as it teaches us to appreciate life's fluctuations without getting lost in extremes. This mindful living, supported by a balanced view, leads to deeper self-awareness and enriched life experiences, benefiting both mental and spiritual well-being.

Acceptance of duality also naturally leads to increased resilience against external judgments. When we accept that every situation and opinion has opposing aspects, we become less vulnerable to the sway of societal norms and expectations. This resilience empowers us to stay true to our values and beliefs, irrespective of external pressures, contributing to stronger mental health.

Imagine someone pursuing an unconventional career path met with both admiration and skepticism. With a firm grasp of duality, they understand that both types of feedback are inevitable and part of the same reality. This understanding fortifies them against discouragement and bolsters their determination.

Resilience in the face of judgment allows individuals to pursue their passions and goals with unwavering focus, unaffected by the variability of public opinion.

In addition, resilience cultivated through acceptance of duality supports personal growth. Challenges and criticisms become opportunities for learning rather than sources of distress. This constructive response to adversity enables continuous improvement and adaptation, integral to mental and emotional development. Embracing duality thus serves as a powerful tool for navigating life's vicissitudes, ensuring steady progress toward personal fulfillment and mental well-being.

Duality in Decision-Making and Harmony

Recognizing life's continuum helps us see both extremes clearly. When we understand that life isn't black and white but instead exists on a spectrum, it becomes easier to identify the nuances between opposites. This clarity can significantly enhance our decision-making process. For instance, knowing the potential highs and lows of an investment helps in making informed financial choices rather than decisions driven by fear or greed.

Moreover, seeing the continuum enables us to anticipate the shifts between these extremes and prepare accordingly. By recognizing that joy often comes with sorrow and success may follow failure, we can plan our actions more effectively. Preparedness for these opposite outcomes not only makes us resilient but also equips us to handle changes without being caught off guard.

This awareness fosters a balanced outlook, allowing us to make decisions that are neither overly cautious nor recklessly bold. Instead, they are well-considered and grounded in reality. For example, in personal relationships, understanding the ebb and flow of emotions can help in navigating conflicts and fostering deeper connections.

Preparedness for opposite outcomes allows for adaptive behavior. Being mentally prepared for both positive and negative results creates a flexible mindset. When we accept that things might not always go as planned, we can adapt our strategies quickly and efficiently. This adaptability is crucial in environments like business and health, where unexpected events can cause significant disruptions.

Such readiness also encourages us to develop contingency plans, which act as safety nets during unforeseen circumstances. In professional settings, having backup plans ensures continuity and stability, even when primary plans fail. This proactive approach reduces stress and increases the likelihood of achieving long-term goals.

Furthermore, embracing duality and being prepared for opposite outcomes nurtures emotional resilience. When faced with setbacks, this mindset helps us recover faster and view challenges as opportunities for growth rather than insurmountable obstacles. This shift in perspective empowers us to face uncertainties with confidence and poise.

Awareness of duality prevents unintended consequences through informed choices. When we fully appreciate the dual nature of situations, we can foresee the potential repercussions of our actions. This foresight is vital in making responsible decisions that consider both immediate and long-term effects. For example, understanding the environmental impact of our consumption habits can guide us toward more sustainable living.

Additionally, recognizing duality helps in weighing the pros and cons more effectively. In decision-making processes, being aware of both sides of the coin allows us to evaluate options thoroughly and choose paths that align with our values and objectives. This holistic view minimizes the risk of negative fallout from hasty or uninformed decisions.

In essence, this informed awareness cultivates a thoughtful approach to decision-making. It reminds us that our actions have broader implications and encourages us to think ahead. Whether in personal endeavors or community participation, being mindful of dualities ensures that our choices contribute positively to overall well-being and harmony.

A clear perspective on duality fosters living in harmony with life's uncertainties. Understanding that life is inherently dual allows us to embrace its unpredictable nature with grace. This acceptance mitigates the anxiety that often accompanies uncertainty, providing a sense of calm and stability amidst chaos. For instance, acknowledging that career successes and failures are part of a larger journey can reduce the pressure to constantly perform.

Living with this perspective also means accepting that difficulties are integral to the human experience. Instead of resisting challenges, we learn to navigate them as natural components of life's rhythm. This approach promotes emotional balance and psychological resilience, making it easier to maintain mental health during turbulent times.

Philosophical and Literary Perspectives on Duality

Philosophers like Albert Camus and Friedrich Nietzsche confronted life's ambiguities courageously. Camus, a prominent existentialist, delved into the absurdity of human existence. In "The Myth of Sisyphus," he explores the idea that life is inherently meaningless, yet he encourages individuals to find personal meaning amidst this chaos. For him, the struggle itself toward the heights is enough to fill a man's heart. This approach invites us to embrace our journey and derive satisfaction from our efforts, regardless of the ultimate outcome.

Nietzsche, on the other hand, introduced the concept of the Übermensch in "Thus Spoke Zarathustra." He challenged the prevalent moral values and encouraged individuals to create their own paths and meanings. Nietzsche's notion of eternal recurrence, which posits that all events will recur infinitely, pushes one to live authentically and fully. By embracing this cyclical view, we are urged to act in ways that align with our true selves, acknowledging the duality of joy and sorrow as integral parts of our existence.

Both philosophers offer profound insights into how acceptance and understanding of life's inherent contradictions can empower individuals. Their works challenge us to face life's uncertainties with a sense of purpose and resilience. Through their philosophies, we learn that duality is not something to be feared or avoided but rather understood and integrated into our lives to achieve a deeper sense of fulfillment.

Literary works by Franz Kafka and Samuel Beckett depict humanity's complexity through duality. Kafka's stories often delve into themes of alienation, existential dread, and the surreal nature of human existence. In "The Metamorphosis," Gregor Samsa's transformation into a giant insect symbolizes the grotesque reality of his life and familial relationships. The narrative oscillates between moments of bizarre absurdity and poignant reflection, highlighting the dual facets of human experience.

Samuel Beckett's "Waiting for Godot" presents a stark portrayal of life's existential uncertainties. The play's protagonists, Vladimir and Estragon, engage in repetitive, seemingly purposeless actions while waiting for someone who never arrives. This duality— hope versus despair, action versus inaction—is reflected in their dialogue and behavior. Beckett masterfully uses minimalism to emphasize the stark contrast between expectation and reality, pushing readers to confront the void within their own lives.

Engaging with these thinkers enriches our understanding of life's perplexities. Through their works, readers encounter the multifaceted nature of human existence. These narratives do not provide clear solutions but rather encourage introspection and acceptance of ambiguity. Kafka and Beckett, through their exploration of duality, provide a lens through which we can examine our own experiences and derive meaning from the seemingly contradictory aspects of life.

These materials offer invaluable insights into human cognition. Philosophical and literary explorations of duality illuminate the complexities of the human mind. They demonstrate how embracing contradictions can lead to greater self-awareness and psychological resilience. By engaging with the thoughts and narratives of Camus, Nietzsche, Kafka, and Beckett, we gain a richer understanding of how our minds grapple with the ambiguities and paradoxes inherent in our existence.

Furthermore, these works highlight the importance of critical thinking and reflection. They encourage readers to question accepted norms and beliefs, fostering a more nuanced and comprehensive perspective on life. This intellectual exercise promotes mental flexibility and adaptability, essential traits for navigating the uncertainties and challenges we face.

Liberation Through Embracing Duality

Finding freedom and joy in life often begins with releasing our rigid perceptions. When we cling too tightly to predefined notions of how things should be, we limit our ability to experience the fullness of life. Letting go of these strict parameters allows us to open ourselves up to life's mysteries. By embracing this openness, we can explore new perspectives and possibilities that were previously obscured by our narrow viewpoints. This shift not only enhances our understanding but also enriches our experiences by infusing them with a sense of awe and wonder.

Moreover, embracing life's dualities enables us to adopt a more whimsical and adventurous approach to challenges. Instead of fearing the unknown or avoiding difficulties, we can see them as opportunities for growth and exploration. This adventurous spirit can lead to personal development and a deeper sense of satisfaction. The unpredictability of life becomes less daunting and more exciting, transforming our mindset from one of apprehension to one of curiosity. As we navigate through life's ups and downs, this attitude helps us remain resilient and adaptable.

Laughter, a simple yet profound human experience, plays an essential role when facing life's dualities. It's a universal language that transcends barriers and connects people. When we laugh in response to life's paradoxes, we acknowledge the shared human condition of dealing with uncertainties and contradictions. This shared laughter creates bonds and fosters empathy, reminding us that we are not alone in navigating life's complexities. Through humor, we can find relief from stress and cultivate a joyful perspective, even in the face of adversity.

Recognizing that life oscillates between certainties and mysteries brings about a profound sense of liberation. We often yearn for stability and clear answers, but the reality is that life is a blend of knowns and unknowns. By accepting this dynamic, we free ourselves from the relentless pursuit of certainty. This acceptance doesn't mean we stop seeking understanding; instead, it means we become comfortable with ambiguity. This comfort allows us to live more fully in the present moment without being weighed down by the need to control or predict every aspect of our lives.

Releasing rigid perceptions goes hand in hand with mindfulness, where we focus on experiencing the present moment without judgment. This practice helps us appreciate the beauty in everyday occurrences that might otherwise go unnoticed. It encourages us to engage with life more deeply, enriching our interactions and broadening our horizons. Being mindful of life's dualities helps us see that there is value in both the light and dark aspects of existence. This balanced view promotes emotional well-being and leads to a more fulfilling life.

An adventurous approach to life's challenges can inspire creativity and innovation. When we are open to different possibilities, we are more likely to devise unique solutions to problems. This mindset fosters a culture of experimentation and learning, where failures are seen as stepping stones to success rather than setbacks. Embracing duality encourages us to take risks and think outside the box, ultimately leading to personal and professional growth. This sense of adventure makes life more engaging and less monotonous, adding excitement and vibrancy to our daily routines.

Shared laughter amidst life's dualities serves as a reminder of our collective humanity. Humor provides a way to cope with difficult situations, offering a reprieve from the seriousness of life. When we laugh together, we create connections that can support us through challenging times. These moments of joy and connection are vital for building strong relationships and fostering a supportive community. Humor acts as a bridge, linking us together through our shared struggles and triumphs, making life's journey more bearable and enjoyable.

The realization that life is a dance between certainties and mysteries helps us develop a more flexible and adaptive mindset. This adaptability is crucial in a world that is constantly changing. By understanding that not everything needs to be definitively understood or controlled, we can navigate life's unpredictability with greater ease. This flexibility allows us to respond to changes and challenges more effectively, reducing stress and increasing our overall well-being. Accepting this dual nature of life empowers us to move forward with confidence and grace, even in uncertain times.

By embracing life's dualities, we allow ourselves to experience the full spectrum of emotions and experiences. This holistic approach leads to a richer and more nuanced understanding of life. It encourages us to celebrate the highs and learn from the lows, seeing each as an integral part of our journey. This perspective helps us find meaning in both the joyful and challenging moments, creating a more balanced and satisfying life. Embracing duality ultimately leads to a deeper sense of freedom and joy, as we no longer feel the need to fit our experiences into narrow confines.

Unveiling the Transformative Strength of Duality

In exploring the concept of duality in life, we've delved into its significant influence on our mental health, decision-making processes, literature, and overall search for meaning. The understanding that every opinion and experience has its counterpart encourages a balanced emotional state. This balance helps us avoid extreme reactions to praise and criticism and fosters resilience against societal pressures. Duality teaches us that external opinions do not define our worth, allowing us to live more genuinely and maintain healthier relationships.

Reflecting on our discussion, it becomes clear how integral this perspective is in navigating life's inevitable highs and lows. By acknowledging that success and failure, joy and sorrow, are two sides of the same coin, we can cultivate a more stable emotional foundation. This stability not only supports our mental well-being but also enhances our physical health by reducing stress levels.

What should concern some readers is the pervasive tendency to seek validation from others, which can lead to emotional turbulence. The fear of negative feedback often hampers genuine self-expression and personal growth. Understanding duality equips individuals with the clarity to see that both positive and negative opinions are part of a broader spectrum, neither wholly defining us nor diminishing our self-worth. This realization empowers us to stay true to ourselves amidst varying external judgments.

The consequences of embracing duality on a wider scale are profound. When more people adopt this balanced outlook, societal norms may shift towards greater acceptance and understanding. This shift would foster environments where individuals feel freer to pursue their passions without fear of judgment, ultimately contributing to a more empathetic and supportive community.

Philosophical insights from thinkers like Camus and Nietzsche show us that embracing life's inherent contradictions can lead to deeper fulfillment. Their works challenge us to face uncertainties with purpose and resilience, encouraging us to integrate duality into our lives rather than resist it. Literary narratives from Kafka and Beckett further illustrate the complexities of human experience, offering a lens through which we can explore our existence more profoundly.

As we conclude, it's important to recognize that embracing duality is not about seeking simplistic resolutions but about finding harmony within life's complexities. By releasing rigid perceptions and accepting life's continuum, we open ourselves to new possibilities and experiences. This openness can transform our approach to challenges, making them opportunities for growth and creativity.

Ultimately, life is a dance between certainties and mysteries. Embracing this dual nature allows us to navigate its unpredictability with grace and confidence. It reminds us that both the light and dark aspects of life contribute to our journey, enriching our overall experience. In doing so, we find liberation and joy in the present moment, unburdened by the need to control or predict every aspect of our existence.

CHAPTER 5
Being Present

Being present means fully engaging with the moment at hand, embracing it with all your senses and attention. In our fast-paced lives filled with constant distractions, finding ways to be present can seem elusive but is incredibly rewarding. It allows us to appreciate our surroundings, deepen connections with others, and genuinely experience life. This chapter delves into the essence of being present, helping you explore how this practice can offer a liberating sense of clarity and joy.

Within these pages, we will uncover the link between presence and the concept of nothingness—a state where the mind is free from clutter and preconceptions. You will learn techniques to release the burdens of past regrets and future anxieties, enabling a peaceful and focused engagement with the current moment. Through mindfulness practices, conscious breathing, and immersing in life's simple pleasures, you will discover how to cultivate a richer, more intentional existence. Join us on this journey towards experiencing unparalleled liberation, contentment, and joy by truly being present in every moment.

Engaging with the Here and Now

To be present is to wholeheartedly engage with the here and now. It means allowing yourself to sink deeply into the experience of the present moment, feeling each sensation and fully participating in what is happening around you. Engaging with the current moment without distractions is an essential aspect of this practice. In a world brimming with constant interruptions from technology and multitasking, finding ways to focus solely on the present can be challenging but immensely rewarding.

Engaging with the current moment means tuning out the noise and focusing on what is immediate. This might involve putting away your phone during meals, watching a sunset without planning your next move, or simply listening to a friend without thinking about how to respond. Engaging fully allows you to appreciate the depth of each moment, fostering connections and creating memories that are more vivid and meaningful. When you're fully present, you're not merely existing; you're living consciously and intentionally.

Another crucial step towards being present is releasing the weight of past memories and future worries. Our minds often trap us in cycles of regret over what has happened or anxiety about what might come. This mental chatter clouds our ability to live fully in the present. Releasing these burdens can free us to experience life as it unfolds, without the baggage of emotional strife that can anchor us to times other than the now.

Letting go of past regrets doesn't mean forgetting them entirely, but rather accepting them as part of your journey while choosing not to let them dominate your thoughts. Similarly, while planning for the future is necessary, excessive worry can be paralyzing. By practicing mindfulness, you can learn to gently redirect your thoughts back to the present, acknowledging worries and past events without becoming ensnared by them. Techniques such as mindfulness meditation or simple deep-breathing exercises can help regulate this process.

Understanding the intrinsic link between presence and nothingness offers another layer of insight. The concept of nothingness can be intimidating, but it plays a vital role in the art of being present. Nothingness here implies a state where the mind is free from clutter, preconceptions, and endless narratives. Achieving this state creates a blank canvas on which each new moment is painted freshly, untainted by past strokes or expectations of future ones.

This state of nothingness isn't about emptiness; rather, it's about potentiality. When we allow ourselves to embrace nothingness, we open up space for creativity, wonder, and genuine connection. It's an invitation to let go of preconceived notions and to encounter life with a sense of curiosity and openness. This approach encourages a richer appreciation of the present moment, as every experience becomes a unique and valuable event in itself.

Finding genuine liberation and delight in life's purest form is the ultimate reward of being present. Liberation comes from freeing ourselves from the tyranny of time—no longer shackled by what has been or what might be, we possess the freedom to truly live. Joy emerges naturally when we immerse ourselves fully in the moment, savoring the subtleties and marvels that daily life offers.

Feeling liberated involves shedding societal pressures and personal fears that dictate behaviors and choices. When we live in the present, we act according to what feels right and natural at the moment, rather than what is expected or feared. This authenticity is profoundly liberating and leads to a deeper sense of joy and fulfillment.

Moreover, delight in life's simplest forms often appears when we strip away layers of complexity and allow ourselves to just be. Whether it's the delight found in the warmth of the morning sun, the sound of rustling leaves, or the intimacy of a shared laugh, these pure experiences become more vivid and fulfilling when we are present to witness them fully.

Finding Serenity in a FastPaced World

In today's fast-paced world, finding tranquility amidst chaos can seem like an elusive dream. However, grounding oneself in the present moment offers a refuge from the relentless pace of modern life. By focusing on the here and now, one can avoid feelings of being overwhelmed and stressed. Staying present helps us appreciate the simplicity and beauty of everyday moments, providing a much-needed reprieve from the constant rush.

Consider the act of grounding yourself in the present through mindfulness practices such as deep breathing or meditation. These activities serve to anchor our minds, preventing them from wandering into territories filled with stressors and anxieties. Mindfulness doesn't require hours of practice but can be integrated into daily routines, offering significant benefits over time. The subtle shift from being lost in thought to being consciously aware of our surroundings can transform our lives.

Moreover, the process of grounding ourselves impacts our mental and physical well-being. Research has shown that being present can reduce anxiety, lower blood pressure, and enhance overall happiness. When we focus on the immediate experience rather than hypothetical scenarios, we engage more fully with life and derive greater satisfaction from our daily interactions and activities. This enhanced engagement can foster a sense of peace and stability that is often missing in our hectic lives.

Shedding historical regrets and future anxieties is another critical aspect of being present. Many of us carry the weight of past mistakes and worry incessantly about what the future may hold. This burden distracts us from enjoying the now and breeds unnecessary stress. To truly be at peace, it is essential to let go of these mental shackles.

By releasing regrets, we allow ourselves to heal and move forward without the emotional anchors that drag us down. Imagine your mind as a clear sky; every regret or anxious thought is a cloud that obscures the sun. Letting go of these thoughts clears the sky, allowing the brightness and warmth of the present to shine through. This practice requires conscious effort and might involve forgiving oneself and others, yet it brings tremendous relief.

Future anxieties, on the other hand, rob us of our ability to savor current experiences. Worrying about what might happen tomorrow doesn't change outcomes; it only diminishes today's joy. Adopting a mindset focused on the present moment minimizes this anxiety, making room for genuine contentment. This approach does not negate the importance of planning but emphasizes living fully in each moment, free from the fears of the unknown.

Exploring the connection between being present and experiencing nothingness reveals profound insights. Nothingness in this context refers to the state of pure awareness, devoid of distractions and mental clutter. It is the essence of simply 'being,' where one's consciousness is fully alive and attuned to the present reality.

Embracing nothingness involves quieting the endless chatter of the mind to experience a state of complete presence. This state is often attained through meditation or other contemplative practices that help dissolve the ego's incessant demands. When the mind reaches this serene emptiness, we uncover a sense of unity with everything around us, fostering deeper connections with nature, people, and ourselves.

The concept of nothingness may seem abstract, but its impact is tangible. Achieving this state allows us to see things more clearly, unclouded by biases or preconceptions. It grants us the clarity to understand our true selves and life's transient beauty. As we become comfortable with nothingness, we start to value the silence and stillness that come with being fully present, enriching our overall experience of life.

Achieving unparalleled liberation, contentment, and joy through presence is the ultimate reward. Liberation here means freeing oneself from the constant pull of past and future, experiencing life unburdened and fully engaged. This freedom leads to immense contentment, as it aligns us with our true nature and core values.

Contentment derived from presence is not dependent on external circumstances. It stems from within, rooted in the appreciation of each moment's inherent value. This internal contentment fosters resilience, enabling us to navigate life's challenges with grace and poise. By valuing the present, we cultivate gratitude, which enhances our overall sense of well-being.

Joy naturally follows liberation and contentment. It is a spontaneous emergence that arises when we are attuned to life's rhythms. Joy manifests in simple pleasures—like the warmth of the sun, a shared laugh, or a quiet moment of reflection. This joy enhances mental health, strengthens relationships, and infuses life with vibrancy.

The Dynamic Dance with the Moment

Presence as an active engagement with life, as it unfolds, requires a delicate attunement to the subtleties of each moment. By tuning into these nuances, we can experience life in its most vibrant and profound form. This involves observing the small details that often go unnoticed: the soft rustle of leaves in the breeze, the gentle sound of laughter from children playing, or the intricate patterns of light and shadow throughout the day. Such attentiveness allows us to appreciate the richness of experience that each instant offers.

This deeper appreciation leads to a more fulfilling life. When we notice and cherish small beauties and moments of joy, we build a reservoir of positive experiences that can counterbalance life's inevitable challenges. For instance, savoring the aroma and taste of a morning coffee can transform an ordinary routine into a cherished ritual. Each moment, no matter how mundane, holds the potential for discovery and delight if we allow ourselves to fully engage with it.

Tuning into the present also strengthens our emotional resilience. By focusing on what is happening now, we are less likely to dwell on past regrets or anxiously anticipate future problems. This shift in focus cultivates a sense of acceptance and contentment, as we learn to value the present moment for what it is, rather than comparing it to what was or what could be. Such awareness fosters a balanced perspective and a grounded sense of wellbeing.

Overcoming distractions and preoccupations is essential for immersing ourselves in the present. In today's fast-paced world, countless demands vie for our attention, pulling us away from the here and now. To fully engage with the present, we must consciously set aside time to disconnect from these distractions. This may involve creating boundaries around technology use, scheduling regular breaks throughout the day, or practicing mindfulness techniques to center our thoughts.

Mindfulness practices, such as meditation or deep breathing exercises, can be particularly effective in helping us overcome distractions. These practices train the mind to focus on one thing at a time, whether it be the breath, a sound, or a sensation. As we become adept at directing our attention, we may find it easier to let go of inconsequential worries and remain present in the current moment. This ability to concentrate enhances our capacity to fully experience and enjoy life's unfolding events.

Another key aspect of overcoming distractions is developing a mindful awareness of our internal states. Often, we are preoccupied with our thoughts and emotions, which can cloud our perception of the present. By acknowledging these inner experiences without judgment and gently redirecting our focus to the external world, we can break free from mental ruminations. This shift allows us to interact more meaningfully with our surroundings and the people around us, fostering deeper connections and enriched experiences.

Seeing life as a dance against the backdrop of nothingness invites us to embrace the transient nature of existence. Life's fleeting moments, much like the steps of a dance, are ephemeral and everchanging. By accepting this impermanence, we can cultivate a sense of freedom and spontaneity, moving fluidly through the rhythms of life without becoming overly attached to any single moment.

This perspective encourages us to approach life with a sense of playfulness and curiosity. Rather than rigidly adhering to expectations or clinging to outcomes, we can adopt a more exploratory attitude. Just as dancers adapt to the flow of music, we can learn to navigate life's ups and downs with grace and flexibility. This adaptability enables us to remain open to new experiences and opportunities, enriching the tapestry of our lives.

Furthermore, viewing life as a dance against nothingness underscores the importance of presence. Like dancers who must stay attuned to each beat and movement, we too must remain grounded in the present to fully participate in life's dance. This ongoing engagement allows us to respond to the unique demands of each moment, making thoughtful decisions and actions that align with our values and aspirations. Through this dynamic interplay, we discover the beauty and meaning inherent in the act of simply being.

Experiencing boundless clarity and tranquility arises from letting go of past remorse and future angst. Holding onto negative emotions associated with past events or worrying excessively about the future can cloud our perception and hinder our ability to live fully in the present. Embracing a mindset of letting go empowers us to release these burdens, thereby achieving a clearer and more tranquil state of being.

Letting go of the past involves cultivating forgiveness and understanding for ourselves and others.

Acknowledging our mistakes and learning from them without self-condemnation allows us to move forward with greater wisdom and compassion. Similarly, forgiving those who have wronged us frees us from the grip of resentment and pain, opening space for healing and growth. This practice nurtures emotional clarity and peace, enabling us to approach the present with a lighter heart.

Similarly, releasing future anxieties entails trusting in our capacity to navigate whatever lies ahead. While it's natural to plan and prepare for the future, excessive worry can drain our energy and distract us from the present. Developing a sense of trust in our abilities and the unfolding of life, despite its uncertainties, helps us maintain a calm and focused mind. By doing so, we create a foundation for experiencing each moment with greater clarity and openness.

Strategies for Enhancing Presence

Mindfulness meditation is a powerful tool for being present. This practice involves focusing on the present moment without judgment. By sitting quietly, closing your eyes, and paying attention to your breath, you can anchor yourself in the now. The goal is not to clear your mind of thoughts but to observe them without getting attached. As thoughts come and go, gently bring your focus back to your breath. This process trains your mind to stay grounded, helping you appreciate the present.

Through mindfulness meditation, you also become aware of your surroundings and internal states. As you meditate, you might notice the sounds around you, the sensation of your body against the chair, or even the emotions arising within you. This heightened awareness allows you to experience life more fully, noticing details that often go unnoticed in the rush of daily activities. Over time, this practice can lead to a deeper understanding of yourself and the world around you.

Integrating mindfulness meditation into your daily routine can significantly enhance your presence. You don't need to set aside large chunks of time – even a few minutes each day can make a difference. Start by finding a quiet space where you won't be interrupted. Sit comfortably and set a timer for five to ten minutes. Focus on your breath, and when your mind wanders, gently guide it back. With consistency, you'll find yourself naturally more attuned to the present in all areas of life.

Conscious breathing is another effective practice for maintaining focus on the present. By bringing awareness to your breath, you can create a sense of calm and stability. This technique involves taking slow, deep breaths, inhaling through your nose, and exhaling through your mouth. Concentrate on the rhythm of your breath and the sensations it brings. This simple act of conscious breathing helps ground you in the current moment.

The beauty of conscious breathing is its accessibility. You can practice it anytime, anywhere – while waiting in line, during a stressful meeting, or before going to bed. Whenever you feel overwhelmed or distracted, take a moment to breathe deeply. This act serves as a reset button, allowing you to return to the present with a clearer mind. It's a practical tool that can quickly interrupt patterns of anxiety or scattered thinking.

Moreover, conscious breathing connects you to your body. Each breath becomes an opportunity to check in with yourself – to notice physical sensations, emotional states, and mental landscapes. This connection fosters a holistic sense of presence, uniting your mind and body in the here and now. As you cultivate this habit, you'll find it easier to stay focused and engaged, no matter what challenges arise.

Enjoying life's simple pleasures is essential for deepening moment-to-moment awareness. We often overlook the small joys in our rush to meet deadlines and achieve goals. However, these moments offer rich opportunities to practice being present. Whether it's savoring a cup of coffee, feeling the warmth of the sun on your skin, or listening to the birds sing, these experiences anchor us in the now.

Taking time to enjoy simple pleasures requires a shift in mindset. Instead of rushing through tasks, give yourself permission to slow down and appreciate the details. Notice the taste, texture, and aroma of your food. Feel the softness of your favorite blanket. Listen intently to the laughter of loved ones. By fully immersing yourself in these experiences, you cultivate a deeper appreciation for life's everyday moments.

Incorporating rituals of gratitude can also enhance your enjoyment of simple pleasures. At the end of each day, reflect on the little things that brought you joy. Write them down in a journal or share them with a friend. This practice helps you recognize and savor the abundance in your life, fostering a sense of contentment and presence. Over time, you'll find that these moments of mindfulness become woven into the fabric of your day-to-day existence.

Building authentic connections is another vital practice for enriching the experience of being present. Engaging genuinely with others pulls you into the present moment, where real connection happens. When you are fully present with someone, you listen actively, respond thoughtfully, and share openly. This creates a space for meaningful interactions that strengthen bonds and foster deeper understanding.

To build authentic connections, practice active listening. Give your full attention to the person speaking, without planning your response or getting distracted by other thoughts. Make eye contact, nod, and use verbal affirmations to show that you are engaged. Reflect on what you hear, asking questions to clarify and deepen the conversation. This level of attentiveness not only enhances your presence but also shows others that they are valued and heard.

Reflecting on the transformative power of being present and embracing the now.

Throughout this chapter, we've delved into the essence of living in the present moment and its profound connection to the concept of nothingness. Engaging deeply with the here and now, we find that it offers liberation, joy, and clarity, transforming our daily experiences into opportunities for richer connections and meaningful moments.

As discussed earlier, being present involves tuning out distractions and immersing ourselves fully in what is happening around us. This means setting aside past regrets and future anxieties to appreciate each moment as it unfolds. By practicing mindfulness, we can learn to redirect our thoughts and focus on the present, allowing us to live more consciously and intentionally.

Revisiting the idea introduced, the intrinsic link between presence and nothingness provides an additional layer of understanding. Embracing nothingness does not signify emptiness but rather a state of potentiality where the mind is free from clutter and preconceptions. This clear mental space allows us to experience life freshly, fostering creativity and genuine connections.

In our current fast-paced world, the challenge lies in finding tranquility amidst chaos. Grounding oneself in the present moment can serve as a refuge from the stressors and rapid pace of modern life. Mindfulness practices like deep breathing or meditation help anchor our minds, reducing anxiety and enhancing overall happiness by keeping us focused on the immediate experience rather than hypothetical concerns.

While some readers might worry about letting go of past memories or future plans, it's essential to understand that releasing these mental shackles brings significant benefits. Letting go of regrets allows for emotional healing, while minimizing future anxieties lets us savor current experiences more fully. This doesn't mean neglecting responsibilities but rather living with a balanced mindset that values the present.

Consequently, embracing this approach has broader implications. Practicing presence cultivates resilience, contentment, and authentic joy, which positively affect our mental and physical well-being. It leads to stronger relationships and a deeper sense of fulfillment. As individuals become more present, they contribute to creating a more mindful and connected society.

Reflecting on the journey through this chapter, the ultimate takeaway is that achieving unparalleled liberation, contentment, and joy through presence is within reach for anyone willing to embrace the practice. This freedom emerges from shedding the burdens of time, allowing us to live fully engaged and in alignment with our true selves. In turn, this fosters spontaneous joy derived from everyday moments and interactions.

To close, consider the dynamic dance with the moment as an invitation to explore life's transient beauty with curiosity and openness. This perspective encourages a playful and adaptable approach, viewing each moment as an opportunity for discovery. By remaining grounded in the present, we unveil the profound richness of existence, experiencing life's unfolding events with clarity and tranquility. The journey of being present is continuous, offering endless rewards as we navigate the tapestry of life.

CHAPTER 6
Inner Peace through Nothingness

Finding inner peace through nothingness can be a profound journey, offering solace and clarity amidst the chaos of our modern lives. The practice of nothingness invites us to strip away the endless distractions and mental clutter that often cloud our minds, allowing us to reconnect with a deeper sense of calm. This chapter explores the transformative power of techniques such as meditation, mindfulness, and moments of solitude to help individuals find inner serenity. Through these practices, one can create mental space to observe thoughts and emotions without getting overwhelmed by them.

In this chapter, readers will delve into various methods for connecting with inner stillness, such as focusing on the breath during meditation and embracing the natural rhythms found in nature. By understanding how solitude and silence play a critical role in fostering inner calm, individuals will learn to detach from external stimuli and reflect more deeply on their true selves. Furthermore, the chapter will illuminate how mindfulness enables a nonjudgmental observation of one's internal landscape, promoting emotional resilience and growth. Through these insights and practical approaches, readers can discover a sanctuary within themselves, cultivating lasting inner peace.

Techniques for Connecting with Inner Stillness

Meditation serves as a powerful pathway to inner stillness, offering a sanctuary from the constant chatter of the mind. By focusing attention on the breath or a specific object, meditation helps quiet mental noise and fosters present-moment awareness. When the mind is calm, it becomes easier to notice the subtleties of our thoughts and emotions without being overwhelmed by them. This practice can lead to a profound sense of peace, allowing individuals to navigate their lives with greater clarity and composure.

As one continues the practice of meditation, mindfulness naturally emerges. Mindfulness is the ability to observe thoughts and emotions without judgment. This non-reactive stance enables a deeper understanding of oneself, reducing the impact of negative thoughts and feelings. Instead of getting caught up in a whirlwind of emotions, mindfulness allows for a compassionate observation of one's inner landscape. This gentle awareness creates space for healing and growth, fostering a stronger connection to the present moment.

Solitude and silence are essential aspects of the meditative journey. In today's fast-paced world, external distractions often pull us away from our true selves. Embracing moments of solitude and silence helps detach from these distractions, providing an opportunity to connect deeply with the inner self. These moments of quietude are not about isolation but about creating a sacred space where one can reflect and rejuvenate. By stepping away from the noise of daily life, individuals can find a serene refuge within themselves, cultivating a lasting sense of inner peace.

Nature plays a significant role in aligning us with the harmonious essence of nothingness. The natural world operates in rhythms that mirror the quiet stillness meditation seeks to achieve. By spending time in nature, whether it's walking through a forest or sitting by the ocean, individuals can tap into these rhythms and experience a profound sense of tranquility. Nature's unhurried pace reminds us to slow down and appreciate the simplicity of being. This alignment with nature's flow can enhance the meditative experience, deepening our connection to the peaceful core within.

Meditation quiets the mind and fosters a heightened awareness of the present moment. Regular practice helps strip away layers of mental clutter, revealing a clear and tranquil state of being. By focusing the mind on a simple point of attention, such as the breath, practitioners can step out of the stream of habitual thinking and rest in the spaciousness of now. This shift from doing to being is crucial for finding inner stillness and can significantly reduce stress and anxiety.

Mindfulness complements meditation by encouraging a non-judgmental observation of thoughts and emotions. This practice teaches us to witness our internal experiences without becoming entangled in them. By noticing thoughts and feelings as they arise and pass, we learn to relate to them with curiosity and kindness rather than reactivity. This mindful approach fosters emotional resilience and a balanced mind, helping us stay grounded amidst life's ups and downs.

Incorporating moments of solitude and silence into daily routines can dramatically enhance one's ability to connect with the self. Solitude provides a much needed break from external stimuli, allowing for introspection and self-discovery. Silence serves as a blank canvas on which the mind can rest and reset. Together, they create an environment conducive to deep reflection and spiritual nourishment. In these quiet moments, the inner voice becomes clearer, guiding individuals towards a more centered and fulfilled existence.

Nature's rhythms offer a blueprint for achieving inner harmony. Observing the cycles of nature—the changing seasons, the ebb and flow of tides—can inspire a similar sense of balance and rhythm within ourselves. Engaging with nature, whether through hiking, gardening, or simply sitting in a park, can ground us and provide a tangible connection to the earth's calming energy. This natural alignment reinforces the principles of meditation, supporting a journey towards a more peaceful and centered life.

Historical Perspectives on Nothingness and Inner Peace

Ancient Eastern philosophies, particularly those rooted in Buddhism and Taoism, emphasize the concept of nothingness as a profound source of wisdom. In these traditions, nothingness is not seen as a void or emptiness but rather a fertile ground for enlightenment and understanding. For instance, Zen Buddhism teaches that by embracing the void, one can transcend ordinary thinking and tap into deeper truths about existence. The practice of zazen, or seated meditation, encourages individuals to let go of all preconceived notions and immerse themselves in the present moment, thereby uncovering the innate clarity and wisdom that arises from stillness.

These teachings suggest that wisdom emerges when the mind is free from distractions and preoccupations. The Taoist concept of wu wei, or effortless action, further illustrates this idea. By aligning oneself with the natural flow of life and letting go of deliberate striving, one can achieve harmony and insight. This state of being allows individuals to act in accordance with their true nature, unhindered by excessive thoughts or desires. In this way, ancient Eastern philosophies provide a framework for understanding how nothingness can serve as a wellspring of wisdom and a pathway to inner peace.

Moreover, the emphasis on nothingness in these traditions is a reminder of the impermanent and interconnected nature of all things. By recognizing the transient nature of thoughts, emotions, and material possessions, individuals can cultivate a sense of detachment and equanimity. This perspective fosters a deeper appreciation for the present moment and the ever-changing landscape of life. Through practices such as meditation and mindfulness, one can develop the ability to find tranquility amidst the flux of existence and draw upon the timeless wisdom that resides within nothingness.

In modern mindfulness practices, the concept of nothingness is often highlighted as a means of achieving inner liberation. Mindfulness encourages individuals to observe their thoughts and emotions without judgment, allowing them to pass like clouds in the sky. By doing so, one can create mental space and detach from the constant chatter of the mind. This practice helps to dissolve the barriers that prevent us from experiencing true freedom and inner peace.

The process of observing without attachment enables individuals to break free from habitual patterns of thinking and behavior. When we are no longer ensnared by our thoughts, we can experience a sense of expansiveness and openness. This state of liberated awareness is where genuine transformation begins. It allows for a clearer perception of reality and fosters a deeper connection with oneself and others. In this sense, modern mindfulness practices underscore the power of nothingness in facilitating personal growth and healing.

Additionally, the integration of mindfulness into daily life can lead to lasting changes in one's outlook and behavior. By regularly engaging in mindful practices, individuals can cultivate a more balanced and centered approach to life's challenges. This shift in perspective can enhance overall well-being and resilience. Ultimately, the mindful embrace of nothingness offers a pathway to inner liberation, empowering individuals to navigate the complexities of existence with greater ease and grace.

Various cultures throughout history have recognized the transformative potential of nothingness in philosophical inquiries and spiritual development. For example, in Western philosophy, existentialists like Jean-Paul Sartre and Martin Heidegger explored the idea of nothingness as central to human existence and consciousness. They proposed that confronting the void could lead to a deeper understanding of oneself and the essence of being. This engagement with nothingness prompts profound reflection and can catalyze significant shifts in one's worldview.

Similarly, indigenous cultures have long revered the concept of the void or Great Mystery as an essential aspect of their spiritual beliefs. For many Native American traditions, the notion of nothingness is intertwined with the cyclical nature of life, death, and rebirth. It represents both the origin and the return, signifying a place of ultimate potential and renewal. These cultural perspectives highlight how embracing the void can facilitate a profound philosophical transformation and foster a more harmonious relationship with the world around us.

In contemporary times, the exploration of nothingness continues to inspire both philosophical discourse and personal introspection. As individuals seek to navigate the complexities of modern life, the idea of finding solace and meaning in the void remains relevant. By engaging with the concept of nothingness, people can challenge their assumptions, dismantle limiting beliefs, and open themselves up to new possibilities. This ongoing dialogue between various cultural interpretations underscores the enduring significance of nothingness in our quest for deeper understanding and personal evolution.

Finally, discovering inner peace through nothingness involves a journey of self-discovery and enhanced awareness. This process requires a willingness to confront and explore the depths of one's inner landscape. By entering the void, individuals can strip away superficial layers and connect with their core essence. This exploration often reveals insights about one's true nature and purpose, fostering a sense of authenticity and alignment.

The path to inner peace through nothingness also entails cultivating a heightened awareness of the present moment. By focusing on the here and now, one can develop a deeper appreciation for life's simple yet profound experiences. This mindful presence allows for greater clarity and serenity, as individuals learn to navigate their inner worlds with curiosity and compassion. In this way, the void becomes a sanctuary where one can find refuge from the distractions and demands of everyday life.

Modern Applications of Stillness Practices

Meditation is one of the most effective contemporary methods for achieving inner stillness. By focusing on the breath or a specific mantra, meditation helps quiet the constant chatter of the mind. This practice allows individuals to step away from the relentless flow of thoughts and engage in a state of calm. Over time, regular meditation can enhance one's ability to concentrate and maintain focus, even in the midst of daily chaos. This focus is not just limited to the meditation session itself but extends into everyday activities, making it easier to stay present and engaged.

Mindfulness, as an extension of meditation, creates space for the non-judgmental observation of experiences. Instead of reacting impulsively to thoughts and emotions, mindfulness encourages individuals to simply notice these mental phenomena without attachment. This observational stance promotes a sense of clarity and understanding, where one can see thoughts and feelings for what they are— transient events that do not define us. By practicing mindfulness, individuals can cultivate a balanced viewpoint, reducing stress and enhancing emotional stability.

Regular introspection is another powerful tool for fostering inner stillness. Taking time each day to reflect on one's thoughts, feelings, and actions strengthens the connection to the present moment. This self-reflective practice enables individuals to gain deeper insights into their inner world, recognizing patterns and behaviors that may be obstructive to their peace. Introspection does not necessarily mean dwelling on negative aspects; rather, it is about acknowledging and understanding oneself fully, which ultimately leads to personal growth and tranquility.

Personal Growth through Embracing Nothingness

Embracing nothingness can become a profound personal journey that yields numerous benefits, starting with the cultivation of inner stillness. In a world filled with constant activity and noise, finding moments of inner stillness is like discovering an oasis in a desert. This stillness acts as an anchor, providing a sense of stability and calm amidst the chaos of everyday life. When we embrace moments of silence and solitude, we allow ourselves to pause and breathe, offering our minds a chance to reset and rejuvenate.

Inner stillness also plays a crucial role in mental health and well-being. It promotes a state of tranquility that can reduce stress levels and anxiety. By taking time to connect with this stillness, we create a buffer against the relentless pace and demands of modern living. Those who regularly practice engaging with inner stillness often report feeling more centered and composed, allowing them to approach challenges with greater clarity and resilience.

Additionally, inner stillness fosters deeper self-awareness and insight. It provides space for reflective thinking and helps individuals gain a better understanding of their thoughts and feelings. With fewer distractions, one can tune into their true desires and motivations, encouraging a more authentic and fulfilling life path. This process can lead to significant personal growth and transformation.

Detaching from distractions is another powerful benefit of embracing nothingness. Our lives are inundated with stimuli from technology, social interactions, and other external sources vying for our attention. By intentionally stepping back from these distractions, we cultivate a deep presence and awareness. This detachment allows us to fully engage with the present moment, fostering richer and more meaningful experiences.

Implementing techniques like mindfulness can aid in this process. Mindfulness involves observing thoughts and emotions without judgment, which enables us to notice when we are being distracted and gently return our focus to the present. Simple practices such as mindful breathing or body scans can be powerful tools to help ground ourselves in the here and now. With consistent practice, these techniques can enhance our ability to stay present, reducing the mind's tendency to wander.

The benefits of this deep presence extend beyond individual well-being. When we are fully engaged, our relationships improve because we can listen more attentively and respond more thoughtfully.
Furthermore, being present in our daily activities can increase productivity and satisfaction, as tasks are completed with greater concentration and care. This holistic improvement in the quality of life underscores the importance of detaching from distractions.

Observing internal experiences without attachment reveals profound insights about our true nature. By creating a mental space free from judgment, we can witness our thoughts, emotions, and sensations as they arise and pass away. This observation process can deepen our understanding of who we are at a fundamental level and unveil patterns that influence our behavior and decision-making.

Through introspection, we may identify habitual responses to stress or recurring emotional triggers. Recognizing these patterns empowers us to break free from automatic reactions and make conscious choices aligned with our true selves. This insight can lead to a more balanced and harmonious existence, where our actions reflect our most genuine values and beliefs.

Furthermore, observing internal experiences encourages self-compassion and acceptance. As we become aware of our struggles and imperfections, we can learn to treat ourselves with kindness and understanding. This compassionate stance can foster a healthier relationship with ourselves, reducing negative self-talk and promoting greater self-esteem.

Finally, embracing nothingness leads to intuitive knowing, which guides authentic living and aligned actions. Intuition, often described as a gut feeling or inner voice, becomes clearer when the mind is quiet and free from clutter. This intuitive sense can provide valuable guidance in making decisions that resonate with our deepest values and aspirations.

Cultivating intuition involves trusting ourselves and listening to the subtle signals our bodies and minds send us. Practices like meditation and solitude can heighten our sensitivity to these signals, enhancing our ability to discern the right path forward. As we build confidence in our intuitive knowing, we can navigate life's uncertainties with greater assurance and ease.

Aligned actions naturally follow from this process of intuitive guidance. When our choices stem from inner wisdom rather than external pressures, we are more likely to pursue endeavors that bring us joy and fulfillment. This alignment between our actions and our true selves creates a sense of coherence and purpose, contributing to overall life satisfaction.

Personal Growth through Nothingness

Throughout this chapter, we have explored various techniques for connecting with inner stillness and finding solace in the depths of nothingness. By examining practices such as meditation, mindfulness, solitude, and engagement with nature, we have seen how these methods can foster a profound sense of peace and clarity. This journey into quietude allows us to navigate life with greater composure and insight.

We began by discussing the power of meditation to quiet the mind and bring attention to the present moment. This practice helps strip away mental clutter, revealing a clear and tranquil state of being. Regular meditation can lead to a heightened awareness that extends beyond the session itself, promoting calm and focus in daily activities. As mindfulness naturally emerges through continued meditation, it encourages a non-judgmental observation of our internal experiences. This compassionate awareness fosters emotional resilience and a balanced mind, allowing us to respond to life's challenges with greater equanimity.

Furthermore, moments of solitude and silence play a crucial role in deepening our connection with the self. In a world filled with constant external distractions, creating a sacred space for reflection and rejuvenation is essential. Whether through solitary walks in nature or simply sitting quietly, these practices enable us to detach from the noise of daily life and find a serene refuge within ourselves. By aligning with nature's rhythms, we tap into a harmonious essence that mirrors the stillness sought in meditation, enhancing our overall sense of tranquility.

The theme of nothingness also emerged as a significant focus, drawing from ancient Eastern philosophies and modern mindfulness practices. These traditions teach that by embracing the void, one can transcend ordinary thinking and uncover deeper truths about existence. Nothingness is viewed not as emptiness but as fertile ground for wisdom and enlightenment. Modern mindfulness reiterates this by encouraging an observational stance towards thoughts and emotions, helping us create mental space and detach from constant mental chatter.

As we embrace nothingness, we embark on a personal journey that yields numerous benefits. Inner stillness acts as a stabilizing force amidst the chaos of everyday life, promoting mental health and well-being. By regularly engaging with this stillness, we build a buffer against stress and anxiety, allowing us to approach challenges with clarity and resilience. Additionally, detaching from distractions fosters a deep presence and awareness, leading to richer and more meaningful experiences.

Observing our internal experiences without attachment reveals profound insights about our true nature. Through introspection, we uncover habitual patterns and behaviors, empowering us to make conscious choices aligned with our authentic selves. This process promotes self-compassion and acceptance, nurturing a healthier relationship with ourselves and enhancing self-esteem.

Ultimately, embracing nothingness leads to intuitive knowing and guides us toward authentic living and aligned actions. When our minds are quiet and free from clutter, intuition becomes clearer, providing valuable guidance in decision-making. Trusting this inner wisdom allows us to navigate life's uncertainties with assurance and ease, creating a sense of coherence and purpose. As our actions align with our true selves, we experience greater fulfillment and satisfaction in life.

In conclusion, the exploration of inner stillness and nothingness offers a transformative journey toward personal growth and inner peace. This ongoing practice not only enhances our individual well-being but also positively impacts our relationships and interactions with the world around us. As you reflect on the techniques discussed in this chapter, consider how incorporating these practices into your daily life can lead to a more centered and fulfilled existence. The path to inner peace is a continuous journey, inviting us to delve deeper into the vast, quiet sanctuary within ourselves.

CHAPTER 7
Mindfulness and Nothingness

Mindfulness and embracing nothingness is a profound journey towards tranquility and inner peace. At its core, mindfulness involves being fully present in the moment, and aware of one's thoughts and emotions without judgment. This practice enables individuals to experience life with openness and curiosity, free from past regrets or future anxieties. Embracing nothingness, on the other hand, refers to creating a mental space devoid of unnecessary distractions, allowing one to achieve a state of calm and clarity. Together, these concepts provide a pathway to a deeper understanding of oneself and the universe.

In this chapter, we will explore how mindfulness practices like meditation, deep breathing exercises, and mindful movement can help cultivate nothingness. We will delve into the philosophical underpinnings of nothingness, examining its role in fostering simplicity and stillness. Additionally, we will discuss practical steps for incorporating these principles into daily life, highlighting the benefits of reduced stress, enhanced focus, and emotional resilience. Through this exploration, readers will gain insights into how intertwining mindfulness with the concept of nothingness can lead to a more peaceful and fulfilling existence.

Understanding Mindfulness

Mindfulness is the practice of being fully present in the moment, experiencing awareness of one's thoughts and feelings without judgment. This means paying attention to your current experience without getting caught up in memories of the past or worries about the future. It's about accepting whatever is happening in the present with a sense of openness and curiosity. When you engage in mindfulness, you observe your thoughts and emotions as they are, rather than trying to push them away or change them.

The roots of mindfulness can be traced back to Buddhist traditions, where it has been a central component of spiritual practices for centuries. However, in recent decades, mindfulness has transcended its religious origins and found widespread acceptance in secular settings. Today, many people practice mindfulness to enhance their mental health and overall well-being, regardless of their spiritual beliefs. This shift has made mindfulness more accessible and appealing to a broad audience, promoting its benefits far beyond its traditional contexts.

Scientific research supports the numerous benefits of mindfulness, demonstrating its effectiveness in reducing stress, improving focus, and enhancing emotional regulation. Studies have shown that individuals who practice mindfulness regularly experience lower levels of anxiety and depression, as well as increased resilience in the face of life's challenges. By fostering a greater sense of self-awareness and emotional balance, mindfulness helps individuals navigate their daily lives with more clarity and calmness. These findings highlight the significant impact mindfulness can have on our mental and emotional well-being.

Incorporating mindfulness into daily life can be achieved through various practices such as meditation, deep breathing exercises, and mindful movement. Meditation involves sitting quietly and focusing on your breath or a specific point of attention, allowing your mind to settle and become more present. This practice helps cultivate a sense of inner peace and tranquility. Deep breathing exercises, on the other hand, involve taking slow, deliberate breaths to help calm the nervous system and promote relaxation. By focusing on your breath, you can create a sense of grounding and presence in the moment.

Mindful movement, such as yoga or tai chi, combines physical activity with mindfulness to create a holistic approach to well-being. These practices encourage you to pay attention to the sensations in your body and the rhythm of your breath, helping to foster a deeper connection between your mind and body. By moving mindfully, you can develop greater body awareness and reduce physical tension. These mindfulness practices offer practical tools for incorporating mindfulness into your daily routine, enhancing your overall sense of well-being and inner peace.

The Concept of Embracing Nothingness

Nothingness refers to a state of emptiness or void, free from distractions and cluttered thoughts. It is a mental space where noise and chaos do not intrude. This concept might seem abstract or even intimidating at first, but it is essential for cultivating tranquility and inner peace. Embracing nothingness requires letting go of incessant mental chatter, creating an empty canvas within the mind.

Achieving this state isn't about literal emptiness but rather a focused absence of unnecessary distractions. Imagine sitting quietly in nature without the constant buzz of notifications and obligations. In such moments, you begin to notice the subtle sounds of rustling leaves or distant bird calls, which were previously drowned out by the din of daily life. This clarity allows you to experience a pure form of presence, untainted by external pressures.

The process of reaching nothingness often involves intentional practices to clear the mind. One common misconception is that this state means thinking about absolutely nothing, which is nearly impossible. Instead, it's about becoming aware of one's thoughts and gently letting go of those that serve no constructive purpose. Over time, this practice can lead to a deeper personal insight and a profound sense of calm.

Philosophically, nothingness highlights the importance of silence, stillness, and simplicity in achieving inner peace. Silence is not just the absence of sound, but a mindful retreat from the constant barrage of sensory input. This quietness opens the door to listening more intently—not just to others, but to oneself as well. Stillness, like silence, involves pausing and appreciating the present moment without feeling compelled to constantly act or react.

Simplicity emerges naturally when silence and stillness are embraced. By stripping away the nonessential, you uncover what truly matters: your genuine thoughts and feelings. This simplicity does not mean deprivation but rather a conscious choice. When you focus on fewer things, you find deeper meaning and satisfaction in each one. This minimalist approach fosters a rich inner life, where distractions lose their power over your peace of mind.

In practical terms, incorporating these philosophical principles into your life involves setting aside regular periods for reflection and solitude. You might start with just a few minutes each day, gradually building up to longer sessions. The goal is to create a habit of mind where silence, stillness, and simplicity are not foreign or uncomfortable states but welcome refuges that enhance your overall well-being.

In Zen Buddhism, embracing nothingness, or 'mu,' is seen as a pathway to enlightenment and self-realization. The term 'mu' translates to 'not' or 'void,' pointing towards the essence of absence. In Zen practice, this is not merely conceptual but experiential, inviting practitioners to immerse themselves fully in the moment devoid of past regrets or future anxieties.

Meditation is a primary tool in this journey, serving as both the vehicle and the destination. Through meditation, one learns to detach from fleeting thoughts and emotions, observing them without attachment. This detachment isn't cold indifference; instead, it is a compassionate awareness that recognizes the transient nature of all things. This recognition aids in dissolving the ego, which clings to identity and outcomes, thus unveiling the true self.

Another critical aspect of 'mu' involves Zen koans, paradoxical questions, or statements designed to break conventional thinking patterns. For example, the famous koan "What is the sound of one hand clapping?" challenges logical reasoning, pushing practitioners towards a direct experience of reality unfiltered by rational thought. Through these practices, the embrace of nothingness becomes a lived experience rather than a theoretical construct.

Emptiness allows for new possibilities, creativity, and a deeper understanding of oneself and the universe. When the mind is uncluttered, it becomes fertile ground for innovative ideas and solutions. Much like a blank canvas ready for a masterpiece, a state of mental emptiness invites imaginative thinking and novel perspectives. It's in these quiet spaces that inspiration often strikes, leading to breakthroughs in various aspects of life.

Creativity flourishes in environments where it isn't forced or hurried. By cultivating emptiness, you provide room for spontaneous insights to surface. This is why many artists and writers seek solitude to connect with their inner creativity. The absence of distractions allows them to delve deeper into their subconscious minds, where raw, unrefined brilliance resides. From this wellspring of nothingness, unique and authentic expressions emerge.

Beyond creativity, embracing emptiness cultivates a profound understanding of oneself and the universe. When free from superficial thoughts and societal expectations, you begin to perceive the interconnectedness of all things.

This interconnectedness instills a sense of unity and compassion, enriching relationships and broader worldviews. It's an awakening to the reality that beneath apparent separations, there lies an underlying oneness that binds everything together.

Mindfulness Practices to Cultivate Nothingness

Mindfulness practices serve as valuable tools in embracing nothingness, a state where one can find tranquility and inner peace. Meditation is one such practice that helps quiet the mind, creating space for moments of nothingness. By focusing on the breath or a specific object, individuals can let go of distracting thoughts, leading to a serene mental state.

Regular meditation sessions can significantly reduce mental clutter, allowing one to experience a deeper level of stillness. This stillness is essential for embracing nothingness, as it provides a break from the constant stream of thoughts and worries that typically occupy the mind. In this quiet space, individuals can connect with their inner selves, fostering a sense of peace and clarity.

Incorporating meditation into daily routines doesn't require extensive time commitments. Even short, consistent sessions can yield significant benefits. Over time, this practice can help individuals cultivate a habit of mindfulness, enabling them to access moments of nothingness more easily and frequently.

Deep-breathing exercises are another effective way to embrace nothingness. These exercises promote calm and clarity, crucial elements for achieving a peaceful state of mind. By consciously controlling the breath, individuals can slow down their heart rate and reduce stress, paving the way for a tranquil mental environment.

Practicing deep-breathing techniques regularly can enhance one's ability to remain present and focused. This focus helps clear the mind of unnecessary thoughts, making it easier to embrace moments of emptiness. The simplicity of deep-breathing exercises also makes them accessible to anyone, regardless of their experience with mindfulness practices.

Additionally, deep-breathing exercises can be integrated into various daily activities. Whether it's during a stressful workday or before bedtime, these exercises can provide immediate relief and create opportunities for experiencing nothingness. Over time, this can lead to improved emotional well-being and a greater sense of inner peace.

Mindful walking and movement encourage an awareness of the present moment, which is key to freeing the mind from clutter. Engaging in mindful walking involves paying attention to each step, the sensation of the ground beneath the feet, and the rhythm of the body's movements. This practice shifts the focus away from ruminative thoughts and towards the present experience.

Incorporating mindful movement into daily routines can transform mundane activities into opportunities for mindfulness. Whether it's walking to work, exercising, or simply moving around the house, being mindful of each motion helps anchor individuals in the present moment. This presence fosters a sense of mental spaciousness, making it easier to embrace nothingness.

Moreover, mindful movement practices such as yoga or tai chi can further enhance one's ability to remain present and centered. These practices combine physical activity with mindfulness, promoting both physical and mental well-being. Through regular practice, individuals can develop a heightened awareness of their bodies and minds, facilitating moments of nothingness.

Journaling and reflective practices can also help release thoughts and emotions, leading to mental spaciousness. Writing down one's thoughts and feelings provides an outlet for expression, reducing the mental burden of unprocessed emotions. This process of reflection allows individuals to gain clarity and perspective, essential for embracing nothingness.

Establishing a regular journaling routine can create a safe space for exploring one's inner world. By putting thoughts into words, individuals can better understand and manage their emotions, freeing up mental space. This clarity enables a more profound connection with oneself and the present moment, paving the way for experiences of nothingness.

Reflective practices such as mindfulness journaling encourage self-awareness and personal growth. By regularly examining one's thoughts and behaviors, individuals can identify patterns and make conscious changes. This ongoing self-reflection promotes a state of mental spaciousness, where the mind is less cluttered and more open to moments of stillness and peace.

Benefits of Nothingness through Mindfulness

Integrating mindfulness and the concept of embracing nothingness into daily life offers profound advantages, one of which is enhanced mental clarity and focus. In our fast-paced world, our minds are often filled with a jumble of thoughts and distractions. These cluttered thoughts can hinder our ability to concentrate on tasks at hand, making it challenging to achieve our goals. By practicing mindfulness, we learn to acknowledge these thoughts without judgment and slowly let go of them. This process helps clear the mental fog and allows us to focus more sharply on what truly matters.

When we embrace nothingness, we create space within our minds that is free from unnecessary noise. This emptiness is not a void but rather a fertile ground for new ideas and insights to flourish. Imagine sitting quietly, free from the constant buzz of notifications and demands; in these moments of quietude, we find our thoughts becoming more organized and streamlined. This mental clarity benefits not only our personal and professional lives but also enhances our overall cognitive functioning. The reduced mental clutter translates to better decision-making and problem-solving abilities.

Moreover, the practice of mindfulness aids in training the mind to stay anchored in the present moment. When we focus on the here and now, distractions naturally fall away. This presence helps in improving attention spans and fosters a deeper engagement with the activities we are involved in. Over time, this cultivated focus becomes a valuable asset, allowing us to navigate complex situations with a calm and composed mind. Thus, integrating mindfulness and embracing nothingness serves as a powerful mechanism to enhance mental clarity and focus.

Another significant benefit of merging mindfulness and nothingness is the reduction of stress and anxiety. Our modern lives are laden with various stressors, from work pressures to personal responsibilities. Stress and anxiety often arise from an overactive mind that constantly worries about past events or future uncertainties. Mindfulness teaches us to bring our attention back to the present moment, helping to diffuse these anxious thoughts. By cultivating awareness and acceptance, we develop a sense of calm and centeredness.

When we allow ourselves to embrace nothingness, we give our minds a much-needed break from incessant activity. This state of inner stillness fosters relaxation and tranquility. Imagine taking a few moments each day to sit in silence, letting go of all concerns and simply being. This practice not only alleviates immediate stress but also builds resilience against future anxiety. As we become more adept at accessing this peaceful state, we find that our overall stress levels diminish, leading to a more balanced emotional state.

Incorporating these practices into our daily routine creates a buffer against the inevitable stresses of life. Instead of reacting impulsively to stressful situations, we learn to respond thoughtfully and with greater composure. This shift in our approach to stress management enhances our well-being and equips us with the tools to handle life's challenges more effectively. Thus, through mindfulness and embracing nothingness, we achieve a significant reduction in stress and anxiety.

Mindfulness and nothingness also contribute to greater emotional resilience and stability. Life is replete with ups and downs, and our emotional responses can sometimes be overwhelming. Mindfulness helps us become aware of our emotions without being swept away by them. By observing our feelings with curiosity and detachment, we develop a deeper understanding of our emotional landscape. This awareness provides a solid foundation from which we can manage our reactions more effectively.

Embracing nothingness further supports emotional resilience by creating a space where we can process our emotions without external disturbances. In moments of quiet reflection, we gain insights into our emotional triggers and patterns. This self-awareness enables us to approach our emotions with greater equanimity. For instance, during times of intense emotional turmoil, taking a few minutes to sit in silence and reflect can help us regain our composure and perspective.

Over time, these practices build a robust emotional framework that allows us to navigate life's challenges with grace. Instead of being reactive, we become proactive in managing our emotional responses. This emotional stability extends to our interactions with others, fostering healthier relationships and a more harmonious social environment. By integrating mindfulness and nothingness into our lives, we cultivate a resilient and stable emotional state that enhances our overall quality of life.

Finally, combining mindfulness and the concept of embracing nothingness leads to improved overall well-being. Our well-being is a composite of mental, emotional, and physical health, and mindfulness addresses all these aspects holistically. When we practice mindfulness regularly, we develop a balanced mind that is less prone to agitation and more attuned to positive experiences. This balanced state of mind promotes a sense of peace and fulfillment.

Embracing nothingness complements this by allowing us to detach from materialistic pursuits and societal pressures. In the stillness of nothingness, we reconnect with our true selves and rediscover what genuinely brings us joy. This inner contentment translates into a more fulfilling life, as we focus on meaningful experiences rather than transient pleasures. The sense of balance achieved through these practices fosters a harmonious existence, where we feel aligned with our values and purpose.

Additionally, the impact of mindfulness and nothingness extends to our physical health. Reduced stress levels lead to better sleep, improved immune function, and lowered risk of chronic illnesses. When our bodies are relaxed and our minds are clear, we experience a higher level of vitality and energy. This holistic improvement in our well-being encourages us to maintain these practices and continue reaping their benefits.

The Role of Mindfulness in Embracing Nothingness

Throughout this chapter, we have explored the deep interconnection between mindfulness and the concept of embracing nothingness as pathways to achieving tranquility and inner peace. By understanding mindfulness as the practice of being fully present without judgment, we recognize its significant role in enhancing our mental and emotional well-being. Additionally, we have delved into the concept of nothingness, appreciating it not as an absence, but as a focused state free from distractions, which paves the way for true presence and clarity.

For centuries, mindfulness has been utilized, particularly within Buddhist traditions, to cultivate awareness and emotional balance. It has since transcended its origins to become a widely accepted practice for improving mental health. Scientific research has consistently demonstrated that regular mindfulness practices reduce stress and anxiety, improve focus, and foster emotional resilience. These benefits underscore mindfulness's importance in modern life, where distractions and mental clutter are constant challenges.

Similarly, the philosophical idea of embracing nothingness teaches us the value of silence, stillness, and simplicity. Rather than striving for literal emptiness, this concept encourages us to strip away non-essential distractions and mental chatter. Through practices such as meditation, deep breathing, and mindful movement, we can achieve a serene mental state that allows for profound personal insight and creativity. This minimalist approach helps us find deeper meaning and satisfaction in our experiences by focusing on what truly matters.

One might be concerned about the practicality of incorporating these practices into daily life. However, even small, consistent efforts can yield significant improvements. Whether through brief meditation sessions, deep-breathing exercises during stressful moments, or integrating mindfulness into everyday activities, these practices are accessible and adaptable. Mindful walking, yoga, or journaling can also serve as effective tools for creating mental spaciousness and fostering a sense of inner peace.

On a broader scale, the adoption of these mindfulness practices can lead to widespread benefits beyond individual well-being. When more people embrace mindfulness and the principles of nothingness, society as a whole can become more empathetic and connected. The enhanced self-awareness and emotional stability that these practices promote can improve interpersonal relationships and foster a greater sense of community. As individuals find tranquility and clarity within themselves, they are better equipped to contribute positively to the world around them.

In conclusion, mindfulness and the concept of embracing nothingness offer powerful tools for navigating the complexities of modern life. By cultivating these practices, we can achieve a state of calm and clarity that enhances our overall well-being. The journey towards inner peace begins with small, intentional steps and holds the promise of profound transformation. As we integrate these principles into our lives, we not only enrich our own experience but also create a ripple effect that can lead to a more harmonious and compassionate world.

As you continue to explore these practices, consider how moments of nothingness and mindful presence can transform your perception of the world. What new insights and possibilities might emerge from the stillness?

CHAPTER 8
Conclusion

In this final chapter, we delved into the profound concept of interconnectedness—a principle that weaves everything in our universe together. This idea, recognized by scientists, philosophers, and spiritual leaders alike, emphasizes that nothing exists in isolation. Whether it's galaxies or subatomic particles, every element is part of a vast, intricate web. The notion of interconnectedness underscores that even our smallest actions can send ripples through this web, affecting the world in subtle yet significant ways.

Marcus Aurelius, a great thinker of his time, encapsulated this beautifully when he said, "Everything is implicated with one another, and the bond is holy, and there is hardly anything unconnected with any other thing." His words remind us that our thoughts and actions are not isolated events but integral parts of a greater whole. Embracing interconnectedness means acknowledging that our choices impact not just ourselves but everyone and everything around us.

This understanding of interconnectedness extends to recognizing the infinite potential within apparent nothingness. Even in voids where it seems nothing exists, an intricate network of connections binds the universe. This implies that the potential within these empty spaces is available to anyone, anywhere, at any time. Our actions, thoughts, and intentions create ripples—like stones cast into a pond—that influence others in ways we may never fully understand. By being aware of this, we become more mindful of our decisions, knowing they contribute to the collective consciousness.

Acknowledging boundless potential liberates us from the belief that we are limited to predetermined pathways. It encourages us to explore endless opportunities for growth and innovation. To tap into this reservoir of potential, we must adopt an open and curious mindset, breaking free from limiting beliefs, societal expectations, and self-imposed boundaries. This allows us to venture beyond what is known and comfortable.

Consider the immense impact you can have when you transcend these constraints. Picture the inventor who explores the unknown and creates life-changing technologies, the artist who produces masterpieces by embracing limitless creativity, or the entrepreneur who dares to innovate and transform entire industries. In our personal lives, harnessing this potential means committing to lifelong learning, self-improvement, and fearlessly pursuing our passions without fearing failure. Communities and societies leverage this potential to innovate, adapt, and push the boundaries of human achievement.

Recognizing the potential in nothingness challenges us to move beyond the ordinary and embrace the extraordinary. It drives us to explore new possibilities, question the status quo, and unleash our creativity. By doing so, we enrich our own lives and contribute to the ongoing tapestry of human progress and innovation.

Think of nothingness not as a void but as an invitation to create. Envision a blank canvas ready for the artist's brush, an empty stage awaiting the first musical note, or a blank page anticipating the writer's words. These empty spaces hold limitless potential, inviting us to shape them with our creativity and intentions.

Visualize an empty stage bathed in light, where life's theater is set to showcase acts of stunning creativity. In this emptiness, we don't see absence but an opportunity for boundless creation. It's akin to stepping into an unexplored wilderness where each step reveals new paths.

By embracing nothingness, we become architects of our futures, wielding tools to design and build from realms of infinite possibility. Within this void lies the universe, ready to be shaped by our actions and intentions. Imagine an artist before a blank canvas— not intimidated by its emptiness but inspired by the potential to bring it to life with colors and emotions.

Similarly, a musician sees an empty stage as a canvas for melodies yet to be composed. A writer views a blank page, ready to fill it with stories transporting readers to distant worlds.

In our lives, embracing creation from nothingness means turning dreams into reality, pursuing passions, and innovating solutions to challenges. We realize we can transform our circumstances even from seemingly nothing. The idea of creating wonders from the void reveals the remarkable potential within each of us. It invites us to step onto life's grand stage and act as co-creators of the universe, shaping our destinies with intention and action.

Embracing nothingness becomes the source of our creativity, inspiring us to forge new paths, write our stories, and paint our lives with vibrant possibilities. This chapter has offered a deep exploration of interconnectedness, infinite potential, and the power of creating from nothingness. These concepts challenge us to reevaluate our perception of the world and delve deeper into our existence.

Interconnectedness teaches us that we are not isolated entities but threads in the universe's intricate fabric. Our thoughts, actions, and decisions have the power to shape the world, reinforcing our responsibility for collective well-being. By recognizing and embracing the boundless potential in nothingness, we empower ourselves to transcend limitations, innovate, and contribute to human progress. As we venture into this realm, we enrich our lives and the ever-evolving tapestry of humanity.

Recognizing our interconnectedness and the potential within nothingness inspires us to break free from constraints and create something extraordinary. Let us seize this opportunity to explore new possibilities, challenge the status quo, and manifest the creativity within us. By doing so, we contribute to a more innovative, connected, and thriving world for ourselves and future generations.

In the journey of self-improvement, we have navigated through an expansive landscape, gaining valuable insights and tools for personal transformation. The path is rarely linear, often marked by peaks of triumphs and valleys of setbacks. Yet, it is through navigating these terrains that we cultivate a positive mindset and develop mental fortitude.

Throughout this voyage, we have understood the importance of having a growth mindset. This perspective nurtures our capacity to view challenges as opportunities for development rather than obstacles. Embracing this view allows us to see failures not as endpoints but as stepping stones toward greater understanding and achievement. We learned how a growth mindset can transform our approach to goals, making us more resilient and persistent in adversity.

Overcoming challenges has been a central theme, emphasizing that every obstacle presents a chance for growth and self-discovery. When faced with difficulties, it's essential to recognize the silver linings and the lessons they offer. Each challenge surmounted testifies to our inner strength and resilience. By developing strategies to confront and navigate these hurdles, we enhance our problem-solving skills and build a stronger sense of self-confidence.

Self-discovery has played a crucial role in this transformative process. Understanding oneself, including strengths, weaknesses, passions, and fears, provides a solid foundation for personal growth. Through introspective practices, we open doors to deeper levels of self-awareness. This inward journey enables us to align our actions with our true values, leading to a more authentic and fulfilling life.

Emotional resilience equips us to bounce back from adversities. Life's unpredictability can often be daunting, but our ability to adapt and remain emotionally balanced determines how we emerge from these experiences. Cultivating emotional resilience involves enduring hardships and thriving amidst them. It requires a conscious effort to maintain a positive outlook and utilize coping mechanisms effectively.

Mindfulness practice has been highlighted as a powerful tool. Being present and fully engaged in the current moment allows us to appreciate life's nuances and respond to situations with clarity and calmness. Mindfulness helps reduce stress and anxiety, fosters better decision-making, and enhances overall wellbeing. By integrating mindfulness into our daily routine, we pave the way for a more balanced and serene life.

The concept of mental toughness embodies the relentless pursuit of goals despite setbacks. Mental toughness is about maintaining focus, perseverance, and determination even in tough times. It's the grit that keeps us moving forward, ensuring we continue striving towards our aspirations despite the odds.

As we reflect on our progress, it's evident that a positive mindset underpins all aspects of personal growth. Maintaining an optimistic outlook, even when circumstances seem dire, significantly impacts our journey. A positive mindset isn't about ignoring reality; it's about seeing the potential for good in every situation. It empowers us to take proactive steps and fosters a belief in our ability to overcome challenges.

Our journey has illuminated the potent power of a positive mindset, the resilience to overcome challenges, and the grace of mindfulness. Embracing moments of quietude and stillness brings profound simplicity and contentment. Our worth isn't tied to achievements but to our intrinsic self. Through this expedition of self-improvement, let these principles guide us, reminding us of our strength and inspiring us to live with intention and authenticity.

The path to self-betterment is ongoing, with each step offering new insights and opportunities for growth. Let us hold steadfast to the knowledge gained, applying it

with wisdom and purpose. May we embrace each
moment fully, with courage and openness, ready to
evolve into our best selves.